The Linguist and the English Language

The Linguist and
the English Language

Randolph Quirk

St. Martin's Press   New York

© Randolph Quirk 1974

AFFILIATED PUBLISHERS: Macmillan Limited, London
—also at Bombay, Calcutta, Madras and Melbourne

Preface

A good deal of the material in the book (for example, Chapter 4) has never been in print before. In some instances, chapters are adapted from work previously published but have been heavily revised and usually expanded. One or two contributions re-appear in substantially the same form as they took elsewhere. But though the textual history is various, a single theme informs the volume: What are the concerns of the 'language side' in university English departments? Mother-tongue studies have had their ups and downs in the English-speaking countries, and in times of revolt or reaction we have sometimes forgotten the distinction and continuity they have attained. In making some modest effort to set the record straight, I have tried to show by precept and example the rich array of 'growth points' at the present time.

University College London,   RQ
February 1974

Contents

Note to Chapter 1

References within Dickens are to chapter numbers, and the following abbreviations have been used:

BH   *Bleak House*
DC   *David Copperfield*
DS   *Dombey and Son*
ED   *Edwin Drood*
GE   *Great Expectations*
HT   *Hard Times*
LD   *Little Dorrit*
MC   *Martin Chuzzlewit*
NN   *Nicholas Nickleby*
OCS   *The Old Curiosity Shop*
OMF   *Our Mutual Friend*
PP   *Pickwick Papers*

I

Charles Dickens, Linguist

I

The Royal Academician, W. P. Frith, tells us in his Reminiscences of an occasion when Dickens was a member of a dinner party at the modest establishment of another artist friend, Augustus Egg.[1] Contentedly replete, Dickens proposed to thank the cook personally. ' "Let us have her in, bless her! and I will address her in appropriate language." "No doubt you would," said Egg; "but, like most good cooks, she has an uncertain temper, and I shouldn't advise you to try it—she wouldn't understand your 'appropriate language' as meant seriously, and she might resent it in her own language, which, I believe, is sometimes described by her kitchen companions as 'bad language'." ' [2]

No less than good cooks, Professors of English have sometimes been doubtful as to what constituted 'appropriate language'; their students have not always understood it in the syllabus 'as meant seriously', and have been known, indeed, to resent any language at all as 'bad language'. In University English Departments throughout the English-speaking world, 'language' has come to have various specialized meanings. Often, it is linked primarily with Anglo-Saxon studies: naturally enough, when one recalls that the earliest form of our language was studied in the universities for centuries before modern English literature was thought to be a fit subject for university study. One thinks of Archbishop Parker at work in sixteenth-century Cambridge,

---

[1] This chapter is a conflation, revision, and expansion of two earlier studies, *Charles Dickens and Appropriate Language* (Durham 1959) and 'Some Observations on the Language of Dickens', *Review of English Literature* 2 (1961).

[2] *A Victorian Canvas*, ed. N. Wallis (London 1957), pp. 61–2.

Hickes in seventeenth-century Oxford producing the first Old English grammar, the 'Saxon' lectures there, and, as the eighteenth century drew to a close, the foundation of the Rawlinson Chair of Anglo-Saxon. In Durham, there was a proposal—abortive, as it happens—to establish a Readership in Anglo-Saxon more than sixty years before a Chair of English had its first incumbent. In the New World similarly, we find Thomas Jefferson seeking to make Anglo-Saxon studies prominent in the University of Virginia which he founded at Charlottesville. And since, as R. W. Chambers put it, the aim of early Anglo-Saxon scholars was often 'to dig out historic fact from the *Chronicle*, or phrases from homilies which could be turned against the Church of Rome',[3] we get that well-established meaning of 'language' which need have little connexion with the study of English language or literature.

From about the mid-nineteenth century we have another important ingredient in the semantic history of 'language'— the one which yields the sense 'all that body of English literature which condemns itself by not being easily readable without studying the language'. Furnivall, Dean Trench, and Herbert Coleridge sat in committee to devise means of augmenting existing dictionaries, and the Early English Text Society was formed for the purpose of editing texts, especially Middle English texts, not primarily for their literary interest, but so that the words enshrined in them could the more easily be collected and examined by the lexicographer.

But by this time 'language' had a seductive allure of still another kind. During the first half of the nineteenth century, historical linguistic study along one particular line—what might be called the comparative anatomy of the stressed syllable— achieved outstanding successes on the Continent and particularly in Germany through the work of men like Rask, Bopp, and Grimm. Thorpe studied under Rask in Copenhagen and Kemble under Grimm in Göttingen, but even without such influential channels the excitement of the new philology would have communicated itself to students of language in this country, reinforcing their interest in oldest English but also canalizing their interest away from the literature, of which the language was the

[3] *Concerning Certain Great Teachers of the English Language* (London 1923), p. 9.

vehicle, towards comparative phonology of individual sounds. Students of English were soon, as Sir Walter Raleigh unsympathetically phrases it, preoccupied with 'hypothetical sound-shiftings in the primeval German forests',[4] and with, to quote R. W. Chambers again, 'Grimm's Law, Verner's Law, Grassmann's Law, rising in successive terraces of horror'.[5] The 1921 Board of Education Report sums up the position by saying that the 'main concern' of 'the teachers of English language in the Universities during the latter half of the nineteenth century . . . was not with English for itself . . . and their interest in it usually stopped short abruptly after the Chaucerian period'.[6] See further, Chapter 4.

There are good historical reasons, then, for the semantic heritage that 'language' has preserved to the present day, for our firmly associating it with 'learning Old English', with 'pre-Chaucerian literary remains', with 'Anglo-Saxon antiquities', 'comparative philology', 'sound-laws', 'ash one' and 'ash two'. And equally there are perfectly good reasons for having concentrated on these topics, since much needed doing on them, just as much still remains to be done: the branches of study which I have mentioned, and ramifications of them which I have not mentioned, must remain a highly important concern of the linguistic side of an English Department and they must be fostered therein.

Yet the grounds have never been inevitable and compelling for a preoccupation with areas which seem to exclude the most obvious concern of 'English Language'—the modern English which is the vehicle of our main body of literature, which is the world's most important medium of communication, and which is the matrix of our cultural life. There were other traditional English interests in language that might reasonably have been expected to bear fruit at the time when Chairs of English were being established in the nineteenth century. John Wallis, Bishop Wilkins, and Locke—to name no other seventeenth-century figures—had a profound philosophic interest in the nature of the English language, of contemporary speech, and of communication itself, and this tradition was greatly nourished in the succeeding century of reason.

[4] *The Teaching of English in England* (London, HMSO, 1921), p. 218.
[5] *Philologists at University College* (London 1927), p. 9.
[6] *The Teaching of English in England*, p. 219.

James Greenwood sought 'to incite the curiosity of such who would have a clear notion of what they speak or write'; James Harris and others pursued Locke's investigation of the relation between language and thought; Joseph Priestly explored not only the phenomena of chemistry but also the phenomena of linguistic usage and the motives governing an individual's choice of a linguistic form. Horne Tooke expounded a theory of words as compound abbreviations which had a direct influence upon Ogden's Basic English. Bentham was concerned with the social basis of language and drew the distinction—so fruitful for later semantic studies—between the referential and emotive use of symbols. To the lover of mankind, he observes, 'an acquaintance with the powers of language', even when applied to conveying 'information for the purpose of excitation', is 'not without its use: for by the same insight by which the mode of increasing its powers in this line is learned, the mode of repressing them, when and in so far as applied to pernicious purposes, is learned along with it'.[7] And where, taking a less austere view of them than Bentham, could we gain 'an acquaintance with the powers of language' more readily than from the works of such as Shakespeare, Pope, Fielding, or Dickens? May we not regret that from this other tradition of language study the word 'language' in our English Departments did not more widely and speedily acquire some such inviting meaning as 'the *use* of language'?

II

Certainly, there is little evidence that if Dickens himself had proceeded from his blacking warehouse to a university he would have shared the linguistic interests of Miss Blimber in *Dombey and Son*, who was 'dry and sandy with working in the graves of deceased languages. None of your live languages for Miss Blimber. They must be dead—stone dead—and then Miss Blimber dug them up like a Ghoule' (DS xi). Rather, it would have been the sociological, communicative, and literary functions of the contemporary English language that he would have sought to explore: the ones, indeed, that he made his life-study, without benefit of university syllabus. That would have been his idea of 'appropriate language', and he proceeded to make himself master

[7] *Works*, ed. J. Bowring (Edinburgh 1843), VIII, pp. 301–2.

of a language that was sensitively appropriate and responsive to a thousand occasions, and proceeded to operate selectively a linguistic range that few users of our tongue can have equalled, and fewer surpassed.

One scarcely needs to be reminded that the language of Dickens was long held in very poor esteem and that indeed it is still so held in many quarters. Its tendency to be sentimental was noticed as early as 1839 in the *Quarterly Review*, where Dickens was also accused of using 'mawkish, far-fetched verbiage'. While Lord Melbourne deplored 'that low debasing style', Swinburne condemned it as bookish and stagey; Arnold Bennett felt that Dickens had 'no feeling for words', and George Saintsbury was appalled by his 'disgusting rant'. Many have regarded as his most serious defect an undeniable tendency to be melodramatic and to indulge in a rather embarrassing poetic prose, such as that describing the death of Little Nell and the aftermath. There are whole passages that could be set out in a kind of blank verse; for example:

> Some shook the old man kindly by the hand,
> some stood uncovered while he tottered by,
> and many cried 'God help him' as he passed along.
>
>   .   .   .
>
> Old men were there, whose eyes were dim and senses failing—
> Grandmothers, who might have died ten years ago and still been old—
> the deaf, the blind, the lame, the palsied,
> the living dead in many shapes and forms,
> to see the closing of that early grave.
> What was the death it would shut in
> to that which still could crawl and creep above it!
> Along the crowded path they bore her now;
> pure as the newly-fallen snow that covered it;
> whose day on earth had been as fleeting.
>
>   (OCS lxxii)

Many again have been offended by his equally undeniable lapses into a dull, turgid expository prose, unrelieved by imagination or any consideration of 'fit' with the character using it: one might instance especially the 'unravelling' passages towards the end of his novels—Flintwinch's long speech to this purpose in Chapter xxx of *Little Dorrit*, for example. Most of us would accept, too, that his innocent characters often speak an intolerably self-complacent, even pompous English, that the novelist's own persona is often ranting or sentimental, that death speeches are more virtuously poignant than realistic or imaginatively moving:

> The boy raised himself by a violent effort . . . 'Mother! dear, dear mother, bury me in the open fields—anywhere but in these dreadful streets. I should like to be where you can see my grave, but not in these close crowded streets; they have killed me; kiss me again, mother; put your arm round my neck—'
> He fell back. . . . The boy was dead.
>
> (*Sketches:* 'Our Next Door Neighbour')

The portentously sentimental apostrophe or rhetorical question, vulgarized with threadbare imagery, such as the passage that concludes Chapter xxxiv of *Dombey and Son* can be all too easily paralleled.

III

Yet it is timely as well as more rewarding to look at the credit side of Dickens's language. It was more admired than dispraised by his contemporaries: even the climax of *The Old Curiosity Shop* was so effective that we are told of New Yorkers lining the quay-side at the approach of the English boat and calling across to those on board, 'Is Little Nell dead?' Nor was the *Quarterly Review* by any means always hostile. In 1837, a reviewer of *Pickwick* extolled Dickens's 'felicity in working up the . . . unadulterated vernacular idioms of the lower classes in London', and in 1839 the journal again praised this aspect of Dickens's talent: 'Boz is regius professor of slang, that expression of the mother-wit, the low humour of the lower classes, their Sanskrit, their hitherto unknown tongue.' This—be it noted—was written of *Oliver Twist*, the book whose manifestations of slang have been most criticized by recent writers precisely for lack of realism: the book which contains the 'improbable oaths' of Sikes and Fagin. The reviewer in the *Quarterly* is in fact more sophisticated than some modern critics in saying that the characters speak as they ought 'with every appearance of truth' and in approving the way Dickens makes Bill Sikes appear to be 'swearing "words that burn"' when in fact he is 'wrapping up this hero—brimstone in silver paper' and using a cunning 'dilution of humorous periphrases'.

The 1839 reviewer, it would seem, has acutely perceived and been able to share Dickens's own attitude to linguistic realism. He wanted, as he himself says in the Preface to *Oliver Twist*, to convey the true flavour of low idiom without letting the language become actually offensive to the reader—as in 'reality' this speech undoubtedly would be. A modern critic, Monroe Engel, quotes a letter from Dickens to a lady-contributor to *Household Words* in which he criticizes her for writing a slang which is simply a transcript of speech and which has not been through the artistic process of being rendered expressive for the purpose in hand.[8]

We may come nearer to a sympathetic appreciation of Dickens's language if we consider it under four heads: his use of language for individualization; for typification; his use of it structurally; and his use of it experimentally.

On the first of these, little need be said; particular locutions and systems of grammar to individualize his characters are striking, almost to the point of obtrusiveness. Indeed, the use of this well-established dramatic device was an obvious desideratum to a writer who worked by means of serial publication, since it provided the reader with a most immediate means of recall and identification. As in life, so in Dickens's art, speech is an integral part of the personality of each character and a part which we recognize each time he or she appears. Sometimes, linguistic identification is particularly dominant, as for instance with Sam Weller and Mrs Gamp; in fact, comparison of Mrs Gamp's speeches throughout *Chuzzlewit* shows an increasing density of identifying features, indicating an increased interest in this aspect of the lady on the part of author and public alike, and preparing us for her eventual abstraction from the novel to become the central figure in one of his best-known 'Readings'. More generally, however, linguistic individualization is small, and is frequently made through a favourite phrase or some peculiarity of pronunciation or grammar:

> 'Well, Sir,' said Mrs Plornish, a civil woman, 'not to deceive you, he's gone to look for a job.'
> Not to deceive you, was a method of speech with Mrs Plornish. She would deceive you, under any circumstances, as little as might be; but she had a trick of answering in this provisional form.
>
> (LD xii)

8 *The Maturity of Dickens* (Cambridge, Mass., 1959), p. 18.

In which trick she was later joined by Mrs Billick in *Edwin Drood*.

Little Dorrit will serve to illustrate one final point: so individualized is character-speech that it can be used from time to time as a means of identification. Such a use occurs as the main structural feature in the first chapter of Book II, foreshadowing which an underlined note in the number plan reads: 'all the names at last. Not told before'. Book I has closed with the unfortunate Gowan marriage and with the unexpected enrichment of the Dorrits which allows them to emerge from the long sojourn in the Marshalsea prison. Book II opens in an unfamiliar locale with a number of unnamed travellers in the Alps, who have come together by chance and who put up in a monastery. Largely from the conversation, the reader recognizes the Dorrits, the Gowans, and the sinister Rigaud, but the strangeness of the environment to most of the travellers, their anonymity in relation to each other, the Dorrits' attempt to escape their Marshalsea past: all these are reflected in the absence of names for page after page. The reader alone has met most of these figures before, and their recognition is both dramatic and surreptitious. And the surreptitiousness (matching the Dorrit fears about their past) finally becomes still more explicit as one traveller, who casts 'a monstrous shadow', seeks out 'all the names at last' in the visitors' book. It is thus given to Rigaud to confirm for the reader the identities of the travellers—including his own, as he adds his name in the book. The chapter ends with Rigaud going 'to his allotted cell' in the monastery, 'cell' having such ambivalence as to flood our memory with the sinister associations he has had since we met him in the first chapter of Book I in a Marseilles prison, fearing the sentence of death.

More important to Dickens than individualizing, however, was the urge to express a regional, social, occupational, or philosophical typification by language. A character's occupation and way of life colour his language as they affect other aspects of his behaviour also, and from his earliest writings we find Dickens assembling an armoury of jargon for imparting this colour. We have theatrical slang in the *Sketches*; the habits of parliamentary language mark characters in the *Sketches* and later in *Copperfield*; there is the circus jargon in *Hard Times*. The speedy effect of experience upon language is illustrated sardonically in *American Notes* with the reference to the newly embarked passengers

' "turning-in"—no sailor of seven hours' experience talks of going to bed' (Ch. ii). By contrast, the speech of Captain Cuttle in *Dombey and Son* shows the deep impression of a life spent in seafaring. Imagery drawn from occupation is made integral to Cuttle's thinking, and the same is true of Mr Toodle, the railway man:

> 'If you find yourselves in cuttings or in tunnels, don't you play no secret games. Keep your whistles going, and let's know where you are.'
>
> 'But what makes you say this along of Rob, father?' asked his wife, anxiously.
>
> 'Polly, old 'ooman,' said Mr Toodle, 'I don't know as I said it partikler along o' Rob, I'm sure. I starts light with Rob only; I comes to a branch; I takes on what I finds there; and a whole train of ideas gets coupled on to him, afore I knows where I am, or where they comes from. What a junction a man's thoughts is!'
>
> (DS xxxviii)

Railway imagery became, indeed, a favourite medium with Dickens, especially (as in this example) as an exponent of another favourite notion, association of ideas; we may recall that the mind of Mrs General in *Dorrit* 'had a little circular set of mental grooves or rails, on which she started little trains of other people's opinions' (xxxviii).

The individualization mentioned earlier is usually made congruent with the kinds of typification now being discussed. Thus the features comically individualizing Mrs Plornish stratify her morally as well. The fawning, insincere references to humility by Uriah Heep in *Copperfield*, and the similar manifestations of Carker in *Dombey*, mirror the fawning insincerity of their characters. The twisted syntax and images of Flintwinch in *Dorrit* are again typical manifestations of his twisted mind and are congruent with his twisted physique. On the other hand, virtue shines through the pure and obviously sanctioned lexicon and syntax of Oliver Twist or of Lizzie Hexam in *Our Mutual Friend*, despite the social neglect, poor education, and appalling environment endured by these characters, reminding us again that Dickens is not striving after a simple or slavish linguistic realism but after a linguistic congruence with fundamental intention.

IV

A third use of language by Dickens I have called 'structural', and by this metaphor I refer to language functioning rather in a representational than in a descriptive fashion. We shall look at important instances of this below (pp. 19ff); we need mention here only the present participles and present tenses at the opening of *Bleak House*, the systematic, periodic use of the historic present in *Copperfield*, an analogous usage in *Our Mutual Friend*, and the almost rhythmic alternation between present and past from one chapter to the next in *Edwin Drood*. But in addition to major features reinforcing major themes in this way, one finds such structural use of language again and again on a smaller scale for specific, individual purposes. A lexical instance occurs in *Great Expectations* where the novelist's equivocation, thematically necessary to be sustained at this point, has as its vehicle a matching lexical equivocation:

> I saw in this, wretched though it made me . . . I saw in this that Estella was set to wreak Miss Haversham's revenge on men, and that she was not to be given to me until she had gratified it for a term. I saw in this a reason for her being beforehand assigned to me . . . I saw in this . . .
>
> (GE xxxviii)

Pip indeed *sees* in the event all that he says: but his experience leads him (and the reader) to believe that what he sees is correct: in other words, to Pip seeing is knowing, and the book's theme is to show that seeing is *not* knowing. If the author had used the verb *know* or *realize* ('I knew from this'), it would not have been true for Pip and it would have expressly misled the reader. If Pip had said 'I concluded from this', it would not only have given the game away so far as the reader was concerned but would have been out of character in attributing to Pip a maturely sceptical awareness of his world and of his own most grievous limitation. *Saw* is thus both pivotal and structural.

The following passage provides another instance of language as direct structural representation:

> Dora is rather difficult to—I would not, for the world, say, to rely upon, because she is the soul of purity and truth—but rather difficult to—I hardly know how to express it, really, Agnes.
>
> (DC xxxix)

David's reluctant, half-formed doubts about Dora are made explicit in their very half-formedness, and we are given a glimpse of the nearest he can come to precision in his vigorous repudiation of *rely upon*, rightly but confusedly repudiated because *rely upon* connotes for David aspects of reliability which he knows to be out of the question and indeed irrelevant.

In a different way, more ambitious but at the same time less subtle, is the mimetic language insistently beating out the varied but inexorable rhythms of the sinister train in *Dombey and Son*:

> The power that forced itself upon its iron way—its own—defiant of all paths and roads, piercing through the heart of every obstacle, and dragging living creatures of all classes, ages, and degrees behind it, was a type of the triumphant monster, Death.
>
> Away, with a shriek, and a roar, and a rattle, from the town, burrowing among the dwellings of men and making the streets hum, flashing out into the meadows for a moment, mining in through the damp earth, booming on in darkness and heavy air, bursting out again into the sunny day so bright and wide; away, with a shriek, and a roar, and a rattle, through the fields, though the woods, through the corn, through the hay, through the chalk, through the mould, through the clay, through the rock, among objects close at hand and almost in the grasp, ever flying from the traveller, and a deceitful distance ever moving slowly within him: like as in the track of the remorseless monster, Death!
>
> Through the hollow, on the height, by the heath, by the orchard, by the park, by the garden, over the canal, across the river, where the sheep are feeding, where the mill is going, where the barge is floating, where the dead are lying, where the factory is smoking, where the stream is running, where the village clusters, where the great cathedral rises, where the bleak moor lies, and the wild breeze smooths or ruffles it at its inconstant will; away, with a shriek, and a roar, and a rattle, and no trace to leave behind but dust and vapour: like as in the track of the remorseless monster, Death!
>
> (DS xx)

All three of the uses of language touched upon so far are three aspects of a single complex force—Dickens's wish to achieve a multi-functional mode of expression. And it was in the pursuit of this interest that he made his most important experiments. He began experimenting young—appropriately enough, at student age; and appropriately enough, he began with the sounds of living speech as he might have done if he could have gone to the College in Gower Street (where his home had been till 1824), the only university in England where the living English language was studied (cf. Ch. 5). Not that Thomas Gurney's *Brachygraphy* (with the help of which he became a brilliant verbatim reporter) could give him the phonetic insight which the Pitman system— first published in 1837—would have done, but it would be enough to develop in him that sophisticated awareness of the sound behind orthography which makes possible many of his most ambitious effects as well as his various kinds of word-play.

Much of the phonetic word-play is a mere romp. The place appointed for 'The Great Winglebury Duel' is Stiffun's Acre (on learning which, Mr Trot not unnaturally shuddered). In an early, imprudent version of another *Sketch*, an orator is called Mortimer O'Silly-one (a Cockney metanalysis, involving a Wellerian *v/w* shift), after the actual Rev. Mortimer O'Sullivan,[9] and his fun with the Irish patronymic prefix is shown also in the title of his burlesque, *O'Thello*. In *Edwin Drood*, a few lines before the punning of speedy trains 'casting the dust off their wheels', we read of orphans 'glutted with plum buns and plump bumptiousness' (ED vi). But phonetic word-play had often a more structural role in his art. There is a pleasing use of phonetic similarity to match a dramatic equation when we are told that the worldly Mrs Merdle 'concurred with all her heart—or with all her art, which was exactly the same thing' (LD li). The half-crazed grief of Old Chuffey is given an added ironical pathos:

> 'Oh! why—why—why—didn't he live to four times ought's an ought, and four times two's eight—eighty?' . . .
> 'Come, Mr Chuffey', said Pecksniff, '. . . Summon up your fortitude, Mr Chuffey.'
> 'Yes, I will', returned the old clerk. 'Yes, I'll sum up my forty— How many times forty—Oh, Chuzzlewit and Son—Your own son, Mr Chuzzlewit.'
>
> (MC xix)

There is even a kind of *phonétique appliquée*. Mrs General teaches that 'The word Papa . . . gives a pretty form to the lips. Papa, potatoes, poultry, prunes, and prism are all very good words for the lips. . . . You will find it serviceable, in the formation of a demeanour, if you sometimes say to yourself in company . . . Papa, potatoes, prunes and prism, prunes and prism' (LD xli).

[9] See J. Butt and K. Tillotson, *Dickens at Work* (London 1957), p. 47.

It would be misleading, however, to expatiate on phonetics in isolation, since for Dickens—very rightly—mere sounds were not in general to be dissociated from total communicative activity. Dickens's abiding interest was in the act of expression, in whatever aspect and of whatever kind. When the once fact-obsessed Gradgrind softly moved Louisa's scattered hair, we are being shown a man who has never learnt the language for what he dimly now seeks to convey, and we are told that so expressive were such actions in him that Louisa 'received them as if they had been words of contrition' (HT xxix). Even the inorganic world communicates. The flakes of soot in *Bleak House* (i) are seen as 'full-grown snowflakes—gone into mourning . . . for the death of the sun'. 'A bell with an old voice' in *Great Expectations* (xxxiii) is imagined as having 'often said to the house, Here is the green farthingale, Here is the diamond-hilted sword'. In a gloomy street, 'a wretched little bill, FOUND DROWNED, was weeping on the wet wall', expressing itself with two-fold aptness, while the fiery spurts from the street lamps as they are lit suggests that they are 'astonished at being suffered to introduce any show of brightness into such a dismal scene' (LD iii). In some novels, the expressiveness of the inanimate works with a powerful choric effect through dominant recurrent symbols: the wind and the sea in *David Copperfield*, for example —the wind with its 'solemn sound . . . a whispered wailing that was very mournful' (li), 'the great voice of the sea, with its eternal "Never more!" ' (xlvi), (reminding us of *The Raven*, 1845, whose author died while Dickens was at work on *David Copperfield*). Again, the meting out of Paul's young life is represented in the clock taking up and going on repeating Dr Blimber's portentous greeting, 'how, is, my, lit, tle, friend? how, is, my, lit, tle, friend?' (DS xi).

If the urge of the inanimate to express itself could be so compelling, of how much greater moment was this urge in humanity. It is no passing obsession which makes Dickens pause in his travelogue *American Notes* to let us share for some fifteen pages (iii) his excitement and wonder at the skill with which blind and deaf children in Boston were taught to associate objects with signs for objects and gradually acquire a substitute language by generalizing the use of these signs. His writings from the *Sketches* onwards bear constant testimony to an overt interest in language.

The relation between standard grammar and substandard usage is noticed in 'The Boarding House', where Mrs Bloss (to be joined later by a whole gallery of colleagues) had 'a supreme contempt for the memory of Lindley Murray'.

v

Among the manifold references—mostly trivial—to the humdrum mechanics of language, the grammar of the verb is especially prominent as a minor theme. Miss Peecher in *Our Mutual Friend* (xviii) tries to expose the looseness of our indefinite 'they say' by making Mary Anne parse the expression. Tom Gradgrind, with some ironic relevance, runs through the present forms of the 'Verb neuter, not to care', in reply to Harthouse's inquiry about the present as distinct from the past feelings of Louisa (HT xix). But an interest in tense, mood, and verbal action goes much deeper than Lindley Murray reflexes of this kind. Death in Chapter xviii of *Dombey and Son* is matched by a switch from preterite to historic present, symbolizing the way in which time has stopped, the movement of life stifled into silence, 'a hush through Mr Dombey's house'. It has been noticed that verb usage contributes a remarkable effect at the opening of *Bleak House*.[10] For the first page and a half, what there is of action is expressed without finite verbs, as entirely verbless sentences like 'London', 'Implacable November weather' are placed in a network of sentences whose verbs are participles: 'Smoke lowering down . . . Foot-passengers, jostling . . . Fog creeping into the cabooses of collier brigs'. This gives the activity of the whole scene an oppressive simultaneity, a timeless continuum which prepares us for and at the same time is reinforced by both the present tense of the finite verbs when they come and also the endless, futureless present of the Chancery case of Jarndyce and Jarndyce, for which the verb usage turns out to be an accumulative symbol. 'Jarndyce and Jarndyce drones on', we are told, the tense of the verb now joined by a semantic symbolism whose end is the same; the case 'drags its weary length before the Court, perennially hopeless'.

David Copperfield gave Dickens admirable opportunity to in-

---

[10] See J. H. Miller, *Charles Dickens: The World of his Novels* (Cambridge, Mass., 1958), pp. 164 ff.

dulge his interest in the verb, since the first-person narrative invited a Janus-eyed view of events. The narrator is a novelist, but the present record is his 'written memory', quite distinct from his fictions (xlviii), a 'manuscript intended for no eyes but' his (xlii). No historical, step-by-step unfolding is forced on him, therefore: memory and imagination can slide back and forth over the events; he can muse on the later effects of actions without—in terms of the convention—'spoiling the story'.[11] We have already noted that the sea reiterates the forward-looking theme, 'Never more'. The tenth number plan has as the second and final note on Chapter xxix, 'Never more to touch that passive hand', and so it happens that before we learn of Steerforth's treachery we are given the ejaculatory chapter-ending, 'Never more, oh, God forgive you, Steerforth! to touch that passive hand in love and friendship. Never, never, more.' It is noteworthy that the language is planned to be distanced from the chronicle by its elevated nature; however dangerously close to the rhetoric of melodrama, repetition and archaic usage are deliberate at such points, marking the movement away from narrative and at the same time giving the comment an added emotional force.[12]

No less than four of the chapters in *Copperfield* are called 'Retrospect', and in them the sudden switch to the present tense mirrors the halting of time's movement. The first achieves this halting symbolically by verbless sentences like those at the opening of *Bleak House*: 'My school days! The silent gliding on of my existence—the unseen, unfelt progress of my life—from childhood up to youth!' In the sudden absence of a reporting verb, it is as though the onward driving engine of his narrative has fallen silent, and the imperative that then follows, calling for retrospection, may—not too fancifully, I think, in the context of water images—be apprehended as the backward drive of the paddles which brings us to a halt amid the present tenses of static description: 'Let me think, as I look back upon that flowing

[11] Even in novels which followed the historical mode, of course, Dickens reserved the right to stand back from the narrative on occasion and make choric comment: the ninth number plan of LD provides for such a movement in Ch. xxxii: 'Oh! If he had but known, if he had but known.'

[12] Cf. David's reflection on his last glimpse of Emily, emigrating with Mr Peggotty: 'Ay, Emily, beautiful and drooping, cling to him with the utmost trust of thy bruised heart: for he has clung to thee with all the might of his great love' (DC lvii).

water . . . whether there are any marks along its course by which
I can remember how it ran. A moment, and I occupy my place
in the Cathedral' (xviii). This is not the first imperative to have
pulled us up in the passage of time. The pattern of recurrent
retrospects is earlier established in Chapter x, the number plan
having the abruptly ejaculative note, ' "Behold me" &c'. As
David, after his mother's death, is sent off to work in London,
the language forces us to contemplate this moment of time in
all its impact upon a child's imagination which obscurely appre-
hends it as a turning point: 'Behold me on the morrow . . . with
my little worldly all before me in a small trunk. . . . See, how our
house and church are lessening in the distance . . . how the
spire points upwards from my old playground no more,
and the sky is empty!' In his worldly all *before* him and the
spire pointing upward *no more*, we have a double edge and
also a reciprocity admirably indicating the past-future tension with which the novel is concerned and admirably endorsing the sudden emptiness of the sky over his world at this
moment.

But the retrospections in the chapters so entitled do more than
call a halt for contemplation, comment, and evaluation. The
present tenses that follow the call for a halt represent a halt for
only a short space: they subtly change function to historic
presents which allow the narrative to be in fact speeded up; thus
the nine brief pages of Chapter xviii cover several years and take
us from David's childhood to his early manhood. But the speed-
ing up is in a staccato series of stills, the cinematic term fitting
the tenses used and the fiction mirrored thereby of the author
'standing aside', as he says (for instance in Chapter xliii), viewing
himself at a distance. To these systematic waves of retrospective
stills, he adroitly adapts in Chapter xliii the old rhetorical device
of *occupatio*, seeing some of these static fragments of time as parts
(he says) of 'a more or less incoherent dream', only fragments
of which therefore can be recalled: 'A dream of their coming
in with Dora; of the pew-opener arranging us . . . ' and so
follow a dozen paragraphs beginning with *Of* and a participle,
the temporary absence of finite verbs matching the timelessness
of dream-vision. The dream is of his marriage, and the dream
language which represents it is, at one level, of a piece with the
consistently insubstantial language in which is couched all his

relations with Dora,[13] and, at another level, is a convenient form for representing events one remove further from narrative than the present-tense stills in which it is embedded. The dream ends, not with a return to historic narrative, but to the intermediate present tenses: 'We drive away together, and I awake from the dream.' The series of retrospects is now drawn to a close.

And I may bring to a close this discussion of time and tense in *Copperfield* by mentioning Chapter liii, only six pages long, but prepared for in the number plan with a disproportionately large group of notes which begin: '*Three times*—White line before each[14] *Speaks of herself as past.*' Three significant moments of time are considered, but first we have the familiar devices of the retrospect chapters, with a slowing down of the language and an invocation to focus the normally ranging vision: 'Oh, my child-wife'—a frequently-used term which itself symbolizes the two-way tension of time—'Oh, my child-wife, there is a figure in the moving crowd before my memory, quiet and still, saying . . . Stop to think of me—turn to look upon the little blossom, as it flutters to the ground!' We then have the typographical device of white space to symbolize the distancing and discreteness. The narrative which follows is now, as we should expect, in the historic present: 'It is morning: and Dora . . . shows me . . . how long and bright [her hair] is. . . .' Another white space, and we have come to the second moment of time: 'It is evening; and I sit in the same chair. . . .' A third white space, and then 'It is night; and I am with her still. . . .' We need not dwell on the mutual congruence of the morning, evening, night, or the symbolic congruence of the third with Dora's death: more noteworthy are the poignantly apt preterites of Dora's utterances, the more prominent and effective in the now established context of present tenses: ' "I was too young . . . I was not fit to be a wife . . . if I had been more fit to be married, I might have made you more so too . . . I was very happy, very." '

---

[13] 'What an idle time! What an unsubstantial, happy, foolish time! Of all the times of mine that Time has in his grip, there is none that in one retrospection I can smile at half so much and think of half so tenderly' (Ch. xxxiii). This passage again, like so many which are of dramatic or structural importance, is drafted in the number plan.

[14] The last two words are uncertain: cf. J. Butt and K. Tillotson, *Dickens at Work*, p. 167.

VI

In the seventeenth number plan of *Copperfield*, Dickens reminds himself to use the item of information that fevers can cause one to forget a foreign language and revert to the mother tongue of one's childhood.[15] Language learning was no mere academic interest. Lamartine said that he rarely met a foreigner who spoke French as fluently as 'ce cher Boz',[16] and we read in Forster of Boz's claim to a fair degree of skill in Italian after even the first month.[17] *Little Dorrit* is one of several novels which reflect his interest in foreign languages. The care taken to provide linguistic local colour is shown in the number plans, which stress Baptist's omnibus word *altro* and twice cite in French the opening of the song 'Qui est-ce qui passe ici si tard?' which recurs in English on Rigaud's lips. Characters freely speak a transparent kind of French idiom: 'My faith!', 'How do they call him?', 'All the world knows it', 'Death of my life!', 'May one ask to be shown to bed, madame?' With a serious undercurrent of irony and awareness of linguistic problems, much fun is made of the Island Race, confronted with the phenomenon of the benighted foreigner to whom English is inexplicably unfamiliar. In 1844, a letter from Dickens described his servants in Genoa addressing the native inhabitants 'with great fluency in English (very loud: as if the others were only deaf, not Italian)'.[18] Just so, the people of Bleeding Heart Yard spoke to Baptist 'in very loud voices as if he were stone deaf. They constructed sentences, by way of teaching him the language in its purity, such as were addressed by the savages to Captain Cook, or by Friday to Robinson Crusoe. Mrs Plornish attained so much celebrity for saying "Me ope you leg well soon", that it was considered . . . but a short remove . . . from speaking Italian' (LD xxv).

Almost inevitably, in this connexion, we find ourselves recalling the conversation at Podsnap's dinner party in *Our Mutual Friend*.

[15] In consequence, Mr Peggotty is twice made to bring this rather self-consciously into his account of Emily's ordeal (DC li).

[16] See U. Pope-Hennessy, *Charles Dickens: 1812–1870* (London 1945), p. 330.

[17] J. Forster, *The Life of Charles Dickens*, ed. J. W. T. Ley (London 1928), p. 334.

[18] *Ibid.*, p. 330.

Dickens indicates Podsnap's ponderous emphasis in addressing his French guest by giving many of his words an initial capital: ' "How Do You Like London? . . . Londres, London? . . . You find it Very Large . . . And Very Rich?" The foreign gentleman found it, without doubt, énormement riche. "Enormously Rich, We say . . . Our English adverbs do Not terminate in Mong, and We pronounce the 'ch' as if there were a 't' before it. We Say Ritch". "Reetch", remarked the foreign gentleman. "And Do You Find, Sir," pursued Mr Podsnap, with dignity, "Many Evidences that Strike You, of our British Constitution in the Streets Of The World's Metropolis, London, Londres, London?" The foreign gentleman . . . did not altogether understand. "The Constitution Britannique", Mr Podsnap explained . . . "We Say British, But You Say Britannique, You Know" (forgivingly, as if that were not his fault). "The Constitution, Sir!" The foreign gentleman said, "Mais, yees; I know eem". A youngish . . . gentleman . . . here caused a profound sensation by saying, in a raised voice, "ESKER", and then stopping dead. "Mais oui", said the foreign gentleman . . . "Est-ce que? Quoi donc?" But the gentleman . . . spake for the time no more. "I Was Inquiring", said Mr Podsnap . . . "Whether You Have Observed in our Streets as We should say, Upon our Pavvy as You would say, any Tokens—" The foreign gentleman with patient courtesy entreated pardon; "But what was tokenz?" "Marks", said Mr Podsnap; "Signs, you know, Appearances —Traces". "Ah! of a Orse?" inquired the foreign gentleman. "We call it Horse", said Mr Podsnap, with forbearance. "In England, Angleterre, England, We Aspirate the 'H', and We Say 'Horse'. Only our Lower Classes Say 'Orse!' " "Pardon", said the foreign gentleman; "I am alwiz wrong!" ' (OMF xi).

VII

This passage does more than make its sharp criticism of linguistic pedantry and naivety: it illustrates Dickens's never-ending struggle to make full use of the conventions of written English for a precise indication of linguistic form. As one devoted to the stage, as a public reader whose skill in representation moved audiences to laughter, terror, and tears, he knew the importance of 'rising and falling inflection, and a variety of emphatic tonal patterns',[19] of which orthography gave no sign. His characters' speeches are therefore repeatedly accompanied by instructions as to tempo, stress, pitch, rhythm, and other prosodic features, rather like stage directions—which in the *Sketches*, indeed, they often are. In 'Private Theatres', we are told that *Richard III* is 'very easy to do—"Orf with his ed" (very quick and loud;—then slow and sneeringly)—"So much for Bu-u-u-uckingham!" Lay the emphasis on the "uck".' In 'Mrs Joseph Porter', an 'old gentleman, who was a great critic', instructs his niece in playing Desdemona: 'Make a pause here and there . . . "But that our loves and comforts should increase"—emphasis on the last syllable, "crease",—loud "even", one, two, three, four; then loud again, "as our days do grow"; emphasis on *days*.' Outside such theatrical situations, too, similar parenthetic notes appear from time to time, as in the slipshod woman's harangue in 'The Pawnbroker's Shop': 'you wagabond! (loud) . . . He's got a wife, ma'am, as . . . is as 'dustrious and hard-working a young 'ooman as can be, (very fast).' Nor is this feature confined to his early work. An example with 'forgivingly' as a sarcastic note on tone appears in the Podsnap passage just quoted from OMF xi, and we find it in the last novel of all: ' "How are you?" (very shortly)' (ED iii). More strikingly, Miss Twinkleton is credited with

> opining that indeed these were late hours, Mrs Crisparkle, for finding ourselves outside the walls of the Nuns' House, and that we who undertook the formation of the future wives and mothers of England (the last words in a lower voice, as requiring to be communicated in confidence) were really bound (voice coming up again) to set a better example than one of rakish habits. . . .
>
> (ED vii)

Parentheses may also be used as a visual sign of lowered prominence: ' "But Mr Copperfield was teaching me—" ("Much he knew about it himself!") said Miss Betsy in parenthesis' (DC i). Such an indication of a second level of prominence is perhaps seen at its best in *Bleak House* when Conversation Kenge interlards a general farewell message with individual farewells as he shakes hands: 'Then it only remains . . . for me to express my

[19] T. and R. Murphy, 'Charles Dickens as Professional Reader', *The Quarterly Journal of Speech* XXXIII (1947), p. 305.

lively satisfaction in (good day, Miss Clare!) the arrangement this day concluded, and my (*good*-bye to you, Miss Summerson) lively hope that it will continue to the happiness, the (glad to have had the honour of making your acquaintance, Mr Carstone!) welfare, the advantage in all points of view, of all concerned!' (BH iv). Nothing could have illustrated better than these concurrent utterances the polished, conscious rotundity of Kenge's conversation, to which, as we have been earlier told, he himself listened 'with obvious satisfaction'.

For the most part, guides to expression are straightforwardly descriptive, a means difficult to avoid if the required nuance is to be conveyed. One may instance the alternation of tone as Little Dorrit tells Clennam about Maggy in her presence: ' "So Maggy stopped there . . ." said Dorrit, in her former tone of telling a child's story; the tone designed for Maggy's ear' (LD ix). 'Mrs Micawber's conviction that her arguments were unanswerable gave a moral elevation to her tone' (DC lvii). And we find descriptions at times far more detailed than these. Miss Knag in *Nicholas Nickleby* 'was accustomed, in the torrent of her discourse, to introduce a loud, shrill, clear "hem!" the import and meaning of which, was variously interpreted by her acquaintance; some holding that Miss Knag dealt in exaggeration, and introduced the monosyllable, when any fresh invention was in course of coinage in her brain; others, that when she wanted a word, she threw it in to gain time, and 'prevent anybody else from striking into the conversation' (NN xvii).

For certain prosodic features, however, Dickens developed excellent typographical devices, involving slight departures from orthography but rarely indulging in forms which would puzzle or slow down the reader accustomed only to orthography. There is interesting evidence of experimentation with the potentiality of the colon in the middle chapters of *Dombey and Son*. For example:

> They made the tour of the pictures, the walls, crow's nest, and so forth; and as they were still one little party, and the major was rather in the shade: being sleepy during the process of digestion: Mr Carker became communicative and agreeable. . . .
> Warwick Castle being at length pretty well exhausted, and the major very much so: to say nothing of Mrs Skewton, whose peculiar demonstrations of delight had become very frequent indeed: the

carriage was again put in requisition, and they rode to several admired points of view in the neighbourhood.

(DS xxvii)

The opening of a paragraph with a subordinate clause whose superordinate clause is in the preceding paragraph (also common in DS) gives Dickens a mode of implying an afterthought or a comment, whether his own or a character's. For example:

> When he afterwards remembered this gentleman and his equipage together, Walter had no doubt he was a physician; and then he wondered who was ill; but the discovery did not occur to him until he had walked some distance, thinking listlessly of other things.
>
> Though still, of what the house had suggested to him; for Walter pleased himself with thinking that perhaps the time might come. . . .
>
> (DS xv)

Hyphenating syllables enables him to express level stress, as when the footman announces the guests at the Veneering dinner party: 'Mis-ter and Mis-sis Podsnap' (OMF ii), and the device is much used in *American Notes* and *Chuzzlewit* to indicate the stressing of American English: *con-sider, lo-cation, pre-ju-dīce, en-gīne,* and the like,[20] sometimes in conjunction with vowel diacritics as well. Hyphens, together with capital or italic letters, appear in Camilla's 'The i-de-a!' (GE xi), Joe Gargery's 'as-TON-ishing' (GE xiii) and his wife's 'a pr-r-recious pair you'd be' (GE ii), and an example like the latter has been quoted above from the *Sketches*. Dashes in place of hyphens suggest both additional stress and syllabic stretch in Mrs Joe's 'Oh, Un—cle Pum—ble—chook!' (GE iv). Dashes also indicate the 'gasping, puffing and sobbing' of Micawber in what are called the 'inarticulate sentences' of his vow to unmask Heep: 'No more to say—a—or listen to persuasion—go immediately—not capable—a—bear society' (DC xlix), reminding us of Mr Jingle's habitual inarticulation a decade before: 'mother—tall lady, eating sandwiches—forgot the arch—crash—knock—children look round—mother's head off—sandwich in her hand—no mouth to put it in' (PP ii).[21] And again, 'I hardly like to mention', says Walter to Mr Dombey, 'such earnings as mine; but if you would allow them—accumulate

[20] Cf. L. Pound, 'The American Dialect of Charles Dickens', *American Speech* XXII (1947), especially p. 128.
[21] Cf. Bulwer Lytton's illustration of colloquial speech, *England and the English* (London 1833), I, p. 133.

—payment—advance—uncle—frugal, honourable, old man.'
Dickens adds that 'Walter trailed off, through these broken sentences, into silence' (DS x). Yet this pointing device may have
a sharply different function when used in conjunction with explicit description of speech; Ham 'was not crying when he made
the pauses I shall express by lines. He was merely collecting
himself to speak very plainly' (DC li).

As David Copperfield's speech starts being affected by the
wine on what is called his 'first dissipation' (DC xxiv), Dickens
notes first the slurred junctures and transitions that take place in
these circumstances: 'and I said (in two words) "Steerforth,
you'retheguidingstarofmyexistence"', the absence of word-spacing
as neatly symbolizing the slur as the recurrent dash the inarticulate staccato of Mr Jingle. But as David's tipsiness increases, so
does the difficulty of indicating its effects, and we depart further
from orthography in 'Neverberrer', 'Lorblessmer', and the crown-
ing example (of which Dickens takes prior note in the number
plan): 'Amigoarawaysoo?' for 'Am I going away soon?'

VIII

Dickens's willingness to indulge in such phonetic spellings
scarcely calls for illustration: his extraordinary ability to create
or re-create a wide variety of speech, and his ingenuity in expressing this variety by means of free spelling, the use of
hyphens and other devices, are among the features which most
immediately strike generations of readers. One thinks at once
of Sam Weller, Mrs Gamp, and half a dozen other comic figures,
but we must not forget that Dickens can sustain with high
seriousness a complicated linguistic system which is markedly
non-standard in grammar, lexicon, and above all in the visually
represented sounds: the language of Stephen Blackpool in *Hard
Times* is a notable example. These things I must pass, however,
in order to draw attention to something not so frequently
observed: the double thrust of his spelling devices for phonetic
and also visual effect. This was important to Dickens because,
while he knew that his works were read aloud in the family
circle and must be effective as sound, it was through the page
as *seen* that he must make his main impact.

It would in any case have been a hopeless task to attempt a

complete phonetic portrayal: the public's associations of spelling symbols were much too constricting, and we see a constant tug-of-war (as in the representation of Mrs Gamp) between the desire to indicate imagined pronunciation and the need to cling to a basic fabric of orthography to keep the speech comprehensible to the reader. For the most part, he attempted only a guide to some outstanding features of a character's pronunciation, leaving the rest to be supplied by the reader according to his linguistic taste or skill. Dickens was probably not greatly surprised when George Dolby told him in Boston of a man who had just walked out in disgust from the author's own reading of Sam Weller, telling Dolby that he could not believe the reader was Dickens, because 'he knows no more about Sam Weller 'n a cow does of pleatin' a shirt, at all events that ain't *my* idea of Sam Weller'.[22]

In fact, the visual dimension gave his art considerably added scope, since it permitted a highly exploitable tension between sound as uttered and sound as interpreted in terms of orthographic and morphological entities. This can be seen even in the *Sketches*: ' "A shay?" suggested Mr Joseph Tuggs. "Chaise", whispered Mr Cymon. "I should think one would be enough", said Mr Joseph Tuggs . . . "However, two shays if you like" ' ('The Tuggs's at Ramsgate'). Polybius was 'pronounced Polly Beeious, and supposed by Mr Boffin to be a Roman virgin' (OMF v).

Here is a device which may usefully display the impact of linguistic form on a child's mind. Among the treats that Peggotty promises young David at Yarmouth is that he will have 'Am to play with', *Am* representing at once Peggotty's pronunciation and David's morphological association of it, as is made clear by the comment, 'Peggotty meant her nephew Ham . . . but she spoke of him as a morsel of English Grammar' (DC ii). In Yarmouth itself, David segments the dialect forms he hears according to the grid which his imagination and limited experience can provide. He learns of the toll which the sea has taken of Mr Peggotty's family; dying and drowning are brought (importantly for the progress of the novel's symbols) to near identity in David's mind: ' "Dead, Mr Peggotty?" I hinted after a respectful pause. "Drowndead", said Mr Peggotty' (DC iii),

---

[22] G. Dolby, *Charles Dickens As I Knew Him* (London 1885), p. 176.

as though in *shot dead*. The same analysis of *drownded* appears a few lines later, and although elsewhere in the novel it is spelt with the verbal ending -*ed*, in both these instances the ending is given a spelling phonetically similar enough but visually indicative of David's alternative and contextually significant interpretation.

When Joe Gargery says 'she Ram-paged out', the form suggesting that his wife 'paged out like a ram', it is not clear whether this analysis is his or Pip's (GE ii), but there are many cases where the interpretation is certainly meant to be regarded as the speaker's and not the hearer's. Mrs Gamp's version of the word *apparently* is spelt 'aperiently' (MC xlix), a slip which only this member of the medical profession could make. Sissy in *Hard Times* calls statistics 'stutterings', because the one word always reminds her of the other (HT ix).

And one should not overlook a further way in which phonetic spellings may have an impact. The speech of uneducated characters often includes spellings like *ses* 'says', *p'raps*, *wos*, *wot*, and Sam Weller speaks of 'the English langwidge'. Dickens was well aware that such pronunciations were normal for the educated and uneducated alike: they are uneducated forms in spelling only, visually suggesting substandard usage in the context of a convention which represents standard usage by standard spelling.[23] Within the space of a few lines in *Edwin Drood*, Sapsea refers to 'Mr Jasper' but Durdles to 'Mister Jasper' (ED xii).

While phonetic and visual effects formed a basis for portraying speech characteristics, Dickens added to them a formidable range of inflexional, syntactic, and lexical features equally appropriate to the regional and social background of his characters. His success in this matter was noted (as we have seen) by numerous contemporaries who were in a better position to judge than we are today. Nor—as the idiom of even his early lawyers shows, to take but one type of educated speech—was it only a matter of the 'lower classes'.

Dickens aims at fitness to type, usually with success. Even a doctor with the merest walking-on part says 'Now, let us see . . . how our ribs are', and attention is drawn to his conformity to type in the matter of pronouns by the novelist's comment, 'There was nothing else the matter, and our ribs were sound' (LD xiii).

[23] Cf. Dickens's juxtaposition of 'ESKER' and 'Est-ce que' (p. 19 above), 'chaise' and 'shays' (p. 24 above).

B

In 'The Great Winglebury Duel', we are shown how 'waiters always speak in hints and never utter complete sentences'. George Orwell is among those who have noticed the skill and sympathy with which Dickens can make the child mind express itself,[24] and we have seen something of this already. Esther in *Bleak House*, Pip in *Great Expectations*, and David Copperfield are presented as I-figures, compromising in language—more or less subtly—between the maturity at which they write and the immaturity *of* which they write. The orphan Pip muses on the gravestone inscription, 'Philip Pirrip, late of this parish, and also Georgiana wife of the above', and its impression on him, formulaic and half-understood, is shown by his replying to Magwitch 'There, sir . . . Also Georgiana. That's my mother', adding that his father is with her—'him too; late of this parish' (GE i). At that time, indeed, 'I read "Wife of the Above" as a complimentary reference to my father's exaltation to a better world' (GE vii). Young David likewise contemplated words graven on stone. Looking at a wall monument in the church, he tried to think 'what the feelings of Mrs Bodgers must have been, when affliction sore, long time Mr Bodgers bore, and physicians were in vain'. He wondered whether they had called in the local physician 'Mr Chillip, and he was in vain; and if so, how he likes to be reminded of it once a week' (DC ii).

IX

Just as child language in Dickens is a study in itself, so also is what may be called his linguistic criticism. To the several modes of thinking of which Dickens especially disapproved, he recognized a corresponding language. The emptiness of a genteel outlook, repeatedly pilloried, is reflected in the hollow reasons for its linguistic preferences: unhealthy euphemistic periphrasis, for instance, especially in connexion with money. In the inhibiting circumstances of entertaining Estella, Pip speaks of the 'bill paid, and the waiter remembered, and the hostler not forgotten, and the chambermaid taken into consideration' (GE xxxiii), terms which comment ironically on his insecurity and social aspirations. The unhappy self-centred stiffness and formality of Mr Dombey is similarly indicated by the pedantry of

[24] *Critical Essays* (London 1946), pp. 17 ff.

'The register signed, and the fees paid, and the pew-opener . . . remembered, and the beadle gratified, and the sexton . . . not forgotten, they got into the carriage again' (DS v). The genteel Mrs Sparsit acidly rebukes Bounderby for saying 'terms' when he has promised (as, significantly, he acknowledges) that he 'would always substitute the phrase, annual compliment' (HT xvi).[25] Even a substituted spelling may be a genteel comfort: when, in 'The Tuggs's at Ramsgate', the family become rich and 'Mother' and 'Father' emerge as 'Ma' and 'Pa', Simon indicates his own elevation by becoming 'Cymon'.

The mathematical materialism which *Hard Times* subjects to criticism deeply affects the language and imagery: even the syntax takes up calculating postures. The cynical Harthouse says of Louisa and her brother, 'So much the more is this whelp the only creature she has ever cared for' (xix), using a pattern which creates a deliberate echo (carefully prepared in the number plan) when it recurs after several chapters at a more advanced stage of Harthouse's plot: 'So much the less is the whelp the only creature that she cares for . . . So much the less, so much the less' (xxiii). But the language of calculation and materialism is not confined to the speech of the fact-worshippers: it infects the novel as a whole. A note in the first number plan reminds the author to make some such comment on the schoolmaster as, 'If he only knew less, how much better he might have taught much more', the novelist's own judgement thus couched (ironically, as I take it) in the language which the book criticizes as inseparable from the mathematically rigid assessments whose fitting vehicle it is.

In *Little Dorrit* similarly, where the pervading concern is with responsibility, the linguistic reflexes of irresponsibility, the evasion of personal obligation, are on trial along with the moral failure itself. The evasive power of the Circumlocution Office (which reappears in *Edwin Drood* xi) shows this criticism in its greatest intensity perhaps, but the criticism itself is pervasive. Even after abandoning the title *Nobody's Fault*, Dickens used chapter headings like 'Nobody's Weakness', 'Nobody's Rival',

---

[25] A similar correction is made in *American Notes*—'to speak more genteelly . . . "compensation": which is the American word for salary' (ix). The alleged American liking for periphrasis, moreover, is taken as a sign not only of genteelness but of an allied pomposity and ponderousness with which Dickens does not hesitate to link aspects of pronunciation in the unkinder American chapters of *Chuzzlewit*.

and repeatedly flirts with the positive, actual—as it were, onto-
logical—status of such indefinites and abstractions as 'nobody',
'somebody', 'the country', 'Society'. It was not that the Bishop
personally expected Merdle to make endowments but that Society
expected it (LD xxi), and the number plan reads 'Society, Society,
Society', trebly underlined. And as in *Hard Times*, both the
language and the morality criticized infect even the characters
who enjoy the author's sanction: Pancks is given the linguistic
humour of overindulging in the indefinites 'you' and 'a person'
(as in LD xxiii), and even Clennam, who is the novel's mani-
festation of responsibility and its repository of conscience, is
again and again ironically shown taking cover behind the broad
shield of Nobody (as in LD xxvi).

Skimpole's play on 'Somebody' in *Bleak House* (xxxvii) and
Gregsbury's use of 'the people' in *Nickleby* (xvi) come to mind
in this connexion, but the latter is rather to be linked with a
related hypocrisy which venerates the word but deprives it of
referent. Dickens seems to have learnt to despise high-sounding
cant—particularly the language of politics—in the days of his
parliamentary reporting. Many of its features are explored in
'The Parlour Orator'; its transatlantic development is ruthlessly
caricatured in *Chuzzlewit*; it is frequently remembered in passages
otherwise unconnected with such satire. When the stricken Mrs
Joe's powers of comprehension were affected, she was able to
repeat the words *Pip* and *Property*, but, says Pip, 'I doubt if they
had more meaning in them than an election cry, and I cannot
suggest a darker picture of her state of mind' (GE xviii), a
cynicism scarcely exceeded by Disraeli's Taper and Tadpole as
they plan a slogan in *Coningsby*: 'Ameliorations is the better word;
ameliorations. Nobody knows exactly what it means.'[26] It is a
regular symptom of Micawber's retreat from reality that he should
find a sufficient reality in words, relishing their 'formal piling up'
and appearing 'majestically refreshed by the sound' (DC xxi). 'I
remember', says David Copperfield, of another character, 'a certain luscious roll he gave to such phrases as "The people's repre-
sentatives in Parliament assembled" . . . as if the words were
something real in his mouth, and delicious to taste' (DC xi).

---

[26] The two passages are compared by J. Warburg, 'Some Aspects of Style',
in *The Teaching of English*, ed. R. Quirk and A. H. Smith (London 1964),
p. 52.

Contempt for word-magic and for a dangerous reliance on words as a sufficient end in themselves comes out especially clearly in law satire: the contending lawyers in *Bleak House* run their 'heads against walls of words' (i). The recognition that, on certain occasions or with certain types of mind, words are potentially at once tyrannous and anaesthetic, according as their function is circumlocution or what has been called 'phatic communion', is an important ingredient in Dickens's linguistic criticism. 'I don't in the least know what I meant' is a comment made on one social exchange (DC xli), and we may compare the following: 'I was so far from wanting words, that I had only far too many of them. I didn't know what to do with them. I floundered among them as if they were water which I was splashing about' (deleted in proof from DC xxiv).

All this is a matter of fitness to type—moral outlook, social status, age, education; but Dickens attempts more than that in his use of language. Early critics, such as G. H. Lewes, commonly deplored his indulging in types when he might have created characters. Henry James, however, complained that the trouble with the personae in Dickens was that they were not types but individuals.[27] The language of a Dickens character does, in fact, often proceed from typifying and stratifying him to individualizing him as unique—unique, it is proper to qualify (as only relevant to consider), in the world of the novels. We have glanced at some instances in section III above. Sam Weller and Mrs Gamp again inevitably spring to mind: 'For if ever a woman lived as know'd not wot it was to form a wish to pizon them as had good looks, and had no reagion give her by the best of husbands, Mrs Harris is that ev'nly dispogician' (MC xlvi). But their like form a very wide circle. Illustration from a mere walking-on part may again be informative. There is a man called Markham who briefly and unimportantly impinges on David Copperfield's life and who has very little to say beyond things like 'A man might get on very well here'—'meaning himself', the narrator adds (DC xxiv). He is foreshadowed in the number plan only by the words ' "A man" &c', indicating that he has been imagined (with what little imagination was necessary for such a trivial item in the book) entirely and solely as a particular kind of linguistic behaviour. Similar examples are abundant.

[27] See G. H. Ford, *Dickens and his Readers* (Princeton 1955), p. 137.

From *Hard Times*, we recall Sleary by his lisp (being 'troubled with asthma', his 'breath came far too thick and heavy for the letter s' (vi)), and Mrs Gradgrind by her talk of 'ologies of all kinds' (xxv) and 'every kind of ation' (viii): the only parts of Gradgrind's knowledge that have rubbed off on his harassed wife are the veriest linguistic husks of learning and abstraction. In *Little Dorrit*, there is Mr Casby whose 'little repetitions' like 'she bears her trials, bears her trials' Dickens links with his hypocrisy (xiii), just as the cynical twist which Flintwinch gives his words is related to the physical, twisted fact of 'his own wry shape' (xv). There is Mrs Chivery whose characteristic word-order is prepared for in the sixth number plan with the note ' "Since in this house I have been" construction', and whose son in a moment of agitation 'adopted his mother's powerful construction of sentences' and says: 'I shouldn't have given my mind to it again, I hope, if to this prison you had not been brought, and in an hour unfortunate for me, this day!' (lxiii). There is Casby's daughter Flora, who speaks with what is called 'disjointed volubility', never once coming 'to a full stop' and pointing 'her conversation with nothing but commas and very few of them' (xiii).

x

The individuality of a character's language may be reinforced by echoes outside direct speech, as we saw a little earlier in 'There was nothing else the matter, and our ribs were sound' (LD xiii). This appears most effectively in the lively form of exposition which in French is called 'le style indirect libre' (as in Charles Bally's classic article), for which the German term is 'erlebte Rede' but for which English lacks a widely accepted name. It is the form whose discovery and exploitation by Flaubert are discussed so valuably by Stephen Ullmann,[28] but whose extensive and varied use by Flaubert's English contemporary has been well-nigh ignored.[29] Yet we find it echoing speech characteristics

[28] *Style in the French Novel* (Cambridge 1957), especially Ch. 2.
[29] Some welcome attention has been paid to it by L. Glauser, *Die Erlebte Rede im Englischen Roman des 19 Jahrhunderts* (Bern 1948), pp. 18 ff., and T. Yamamoto, *Growth and System of the Language of Dickens* (Kansai 1952), pp. 372 ff. More generally on the treatment of speech, see G. L. Brook, *The Language of Dickens* (London 1970) and N. Page, *Speech in the English Novel* (London 1973), especially Ch. 6.

from the *Sketches* onwards: in 'The Mistaken Milliner', a servant-
girl is said to have spoken of someone who 'was a-going to be
married and Missis was so proud about it there was no bearing
of her',—the tenses converted for reported speech but the forms
retaining the stamp of the speaker's usage. 'They was all hard
up there, Mr Plornish said, uncommon hard up, to-be-sure. Well,
he couldn't say how it was . . . all he know'd was, that so it was'
(LD xii). If it were direct speech here, Plornish would actually
be saying not 'they was' and 'I know'd' but simply 'they are'
and 'I know': but the substandard forms of the converted tenses
are true for Plornish's grammar. Again, the linguistic reflex of
Mr Dorrit's genteel hypocrisy is so insistent that it seems natural
to find it following through into reports of what he said: 'that
people—ha—people in an exalted position, my dear, must scrupu-
lously exact respect . . . Therefore, my dear, he—ha—he laid his
parental injunctions upon her, to remember that she was a lady,
who had now to conduct herself with—hum—a proper pride'
(LD xxxix).

Miss Twinkleton's Christmas oration in *Edwin Drood* is presented in this mode and not in direct speech:

> Hem! Again a revolving year, ladies, had brought us to a pause in our
> studies—let us hope our greatly advanced studies—and, like the
> mariner in his bark, the warrior in his tent, the captive in his dungeon,
> and the traveller in his various conveyances, we yearned for home.
> Did we say, on such an occasion, in the opening words of Mr
> Addison's impressive tragedy:
>
> > 'The dawn is overcast, the morning lowers,
> > And heavily in clouds brings on the day,
> > The great, th' important day—?'

Not so. From horizon to zenith all was *couleur de rose*, for all was
redolent of our relations and friends. Might *we* find *them* prospering
as *we* expected; might *they* find *us* prospering as *they* expected!
Ladies, we would now, with our love to one another, wish one
another good-bye, and happiness, until we met again. And when the
time should come for our resumption of those pursuits which, (here
a general depression set in all round), pursuits which, pursuits
which;—then let us remember what was said by the Spartan General,
in words too trite for repetition, at the battle it were superfluous to
specify.

(ED xiii)

Dickens found that free indirect speech could give him the speed and economy of narrative, as well as potential colouring to suggest (*a*) the characteristic idiom of a particular character, (*b*) the unspoken reflection of a character, again in terms of his own idiom, and (*c*) the impact of one character upon another without either the clumsiness of explanation or the delay and cumbersome loss of continuity that would be entailed if this were done by making the second speak his reaction. All facets of his potentiality are admirably illustrated in the eleventh chapter of *Bleak House* where there is an episode that is almost certainly based upon a report in the *Household Narrative* of an Alderman interrogating a fourteen-year-old boy called George Ruby who was called as a witness in an assault action:

> Alderman Humphrey: Well, do you know what you are about? Do you know what an oath is? Boy: No. Alderman: Can you read? Boy: No. Alderman: Do you ever say your prayers? Boy: No, never. Alderman: Do you know what prayers are? Boy: No. Alderman: Do you know what God is? Boy: No. Alderman: Do you know what the devil is? Boy: I've heard of the devil, but I don't know him. Alderman: What do you know? Boy: I knows how to sweep the crossings. Alderman: And that's all? Boy: That's all. I sweeps a crossing.
>
> (*The Household Narrative*, January 1850, p. 7)

This dull report, rudimentarily enlivened only by distinguishing the boy's speech with a trace of substandard conjugation, is in sharp contrast with the *Bleak House* episode, which is presented entirely by means of free indirect speech.

> ... the boy that sweeps the crossing ... would tell you ...
> Says the Coroner, is that boy here? ...
> Name, Jo. Nothing else that he knows on. Don't know that everybody has two names. Never heard of sich a think.
> Don't know that Jo is short for a longer name. Thinks it long enough for *him*. *He* don't find no fault with it. Spell it? No. He can't spell it. No father, no mother, no friends. Never been to school. What's home? Knows a broom's a broom, and knows that it's wicked to tell a lie. Don't recollect who told him about the broom, or about the lie, but knows both.
>
> (BH xi)

We have a vivid dramatization of Jo and an imaginative rendering of his language but transmuted to a report which lets us share the Coroner's reaction to his words (contrast 'Never heard of sich a think' with 'Don't know that everybody has two names'), and which also perhaps echoes the muttering of the clerk of the court who is entering the deposition ('No father, no mother, no friends').[30]

XI

Not that *erlebte Rede* was Dickens's only device for expressing the complexities and simultaneities of consciousness. Dame Una Pope-Hennessy observes that Flora Finching's idiosyncratic speech in *Dorrit* anticipates the more recent 'stream of consciousness' technique. Some of Dickens's minor writings show his tackling experiments in this direction rather more radically and to a more sustained degree than he does in the case of Flora; one may consider, for instance, the following:

> I am an old woman now and my good looks are gone but that's me my dear over the plate-warmer and considered like in the times when you used to pay two guineas on ivory and took your chance pretty much how you came out, which made you very careful how you left it about afterwards because people were turned so red and uncomfortable by mostly guessing it was somebody else quite different, and there was once a certain person that put his money in a hop business that came in one one morning to pay his rent and respects being the second floor that would have taken it down from its hook and put it in his breast pocket—you understand my dear— for the L, he says of the original—only there was no mellowness in *his* voice and I couldn't let him, but his opinion of it you may gather from his saying to it 'Speak to me Emma!' which was far from a rational observation no doubt but still a tribute to its being a

[30] Despite the obvious differences, it would seem that Humphry House's suggestion (*The Dickens World*, London 1941, pp. 32 f.) that the passages are cognate is perfectly sound. On p. 3 of the same issue of the *Household Narrative* there are Dickensian editorial comments on the incident as witnessing the 'startling depths of mental ignorance and neglect concealed beneath our hollow shows of civilization'; the editorial deplores the magistrate's rejection of the boy's evidence 'as that of a creature who knew nothing whatever of the obligation to tell the truth', when it should have been obvious that for all the lad's terrible ignorance he was completely unable 'to speak other than the truth'. So too in the *Bleak House* episode, Dickens stresses Jo's unswerving truthfulness and makes the coroner's rejection of his evidence preposterous by giving as the grounds that the boy 'can't exactly say' what will happen to him 'after he's dead'.

likeness, and I think myself it *was* like me when I was young and wore that sort of stays.

(Mrs Lirriper's Lodgings i)

One finds the same kind of interest at work in the numerous attempts that Dickens makes to show in a character's speech the interaction of personality and experience, a matter which seems to have been of particular fascination for Dickens if the experience itself is verbal. On two occasions, for instance, he demonstrates the impression made on the unsophisticated mind by a piece of commemorative verse. We have already seen the *Copperfield* example (p. 26). In Ch. xxxix of *Dombey*, Captain Cuttle says of the Missing Walter: ' "Affliction sore, long time he bore, and let us overhaul the wollume, and there find it." "Physicians", observed Bunsby, "was in vain" ', acknowledging a shared culture in respect of this linguistic object.

The interaction of personality with linguistic experience and physical experience is admirably demonstrated in Ch. xviii of *The Uncommercial Traveller*, where the anxious traveller's mind is displayed in simultaneous reaction to a rough night crossing of the English Channel and to the words of a popular song. The effect very much depends on the contemporary reader's being no doubt thoroughly familiar with the words of the song, and since this degree of familiarity may not be omnipresent today, it is perhaps worth quoting the relevant stanzas as written by the indefatigable author of 'The Minstrel Boy', 'The Last Rose of Summer', 'Believe me if All Those Endearing Young Charms', and other pieces which wrung the heart of the mid-nineteenth century:

> Rich and rare were the gems she wore,
> And a bright gold ring on her wand she bore;
> But Oh her beauty was far beyond
> Her sparkling gems or snow white wand.
>
> Lady! dost thou not fear to stray
> So lone and lovely through this bleak way?
> Are Erin's sons so good or so cold
> As not to be tempted by woman or gold?
>
> Sir Knight, I fear not the least alarm,
> No son of Erin will offer me harm;
> For though they love woman and golden store,
> Sir Knight, they love Honour and Virtue more.

(From Irish Melodies, by Thomas Moore)

One may now consider the way this is woven into the traveller's experience and takes on a comically transmuted form in his consciousness:

The wind blows stiffly from the Nor'-East, the sea runs high, we ship a deal of water . . . I am under a curious compulsion to occupy myself with the Irish melodies . . . 'Rich and rare were the ge-ems she-e-e-e wore, And a bright gold ring on her wa-and she bo-ore, But O her beauty was fa-a-a—a-r beyond'—I am particularly proud of my execution here, when I become aware of another awkward shock from the sea . . . 'Her sparkling gems, or snow-white wand, But O her beauty was fa-a-a-a-a-r beyond'—another awkward one here . . . 'Her spa-a-rkling ge-ems or her Port! port! steady! steady! snow-white fellow-creature at the paddle-box very selfishly audible, bump, roar, wash, white wand.'
As my execution of the Irish melodies partakes of my imperfect perceptions of what is going on around me, so what is going on around me becomes something else than what it is . . . Still, through all this, I must ask her (who *was* she I wonder!) for the fiftieth time and without ever stopping, Does she not fear to stray, So lone and lovely through this bleak way, And are Erin's sons so good or so cold, As not to be tempted by more fellow-creatures at the paddle-box or gold? Sir Knight I feel not the least alarm, No son of Erin will offer me harm, For though they love fellow-creature with umbrella down again and golden store, Sir Knight they what a tremendous one love honour and virtue more: For though they love Stewards with a bull's eye bright, they'll trouble you for your ticket, sir—rough passage to-night!

(*The Uncommercial Traveller* xviii)

In this example of Dickens's multifunctional language, it is noteworthy how difficult it is to label the amalgam of expository modes that it constitutes. We have in the first place some fairly simple narrative which described the physical world ('The wind blows') and its impact upon the narrator ('I am under a strange compulsion'). The use of the historic present for this aids the bold juxtaposition of internal monologue ('Sir Knight they what a tremendous one'). But the stages of manifesting consciousness do not end with internal monologue; Dickens uses a reflexive device by which we are given not merely the impressions generated by the narrator's consciousness ('snow-white fellow-creature . . . very selfishly audible') but also, as though indistinguishable from these, utterances from the outside world as they impinge upon the narrator's consciousness: 'though they love Stewards with a bull's eye bright, they'll trouble you for your ticket, sir—rough passage tonight.' The song, which at first maintains its identity and keeps its linguistic distance with the help of quotation marks, soon becomes disturbed by interruptions, though the persistence of the quotation marks represent the traveller's struggle to keep it distinct; presently, however, the song and the rest of consciousness become indistinguishable, and indeed the song imposes its pattern on the whole experience, as we see in the rhyme and metre of the concluding lines quoted. As in the passage presented earlier from *Bleak House*, we have a many-layered, many-faceted language economically transmuting both experience and consciousness into a whole which is rich with suggestion.[31]

Much could be said on other aspects of Dickens's language—the ebullience and creativeness, for instance, his interest in jargon, the symbolism of his names. His sense of the appropriate in language, his awareness that in the use of language we have an index to man's nature and experience, his explorer's interest in all communicative phenomena; it is the relevance of these that I would urge, not only to the evaluation of Dickens, but also more widely to the orientation of English linguistic studies.

[31] So too, in *Dombey and Son*, having once made Carker's teeth emblematic of his wolfish villainy, Dickens can boldly superimpose them on our whole consciousness of this man:

In the office, in the court, in the street, and on 'Change, they glistened. . . . Five o'clock arriving, and with it Mr Carker's bay horse, they got on horseback, and went gleaming up Cheapside.   (DS xxii)

2

A Glimpse of Eighteenth-Century Prescriptivism

Both in the Advertisement (dated 1 August 1814) and in the Introduction (dated 29 May 1818) to his new edition of Johnson's *Dictionary*, Henry John Todd refers to a copy of the *Dictionary* put at his disposal by Messrs Longman and Company, Booksellers, which had belonged to 'the late Rev. Mr Eyre' and which bore his annotations.[1] Not surprisingly, perhaps, little is generally known about Eyre: a fairly uneventful life of teaching and preaching in the Midlands, with however cultivated private interests, did not invite fame, and his likeliest chance of immortality as a man of literary interests seemed doomed when Todd dismissed his extensive notes as yielding 'no great harvest of intelligence' (4th page of Advertisement).[2]

James Eyre, the son of John Eyre of Coventry, was born (according to the *DNB*) in 1748. This is at variance with the *Alumni Cantabrigienses*[3] which gives his age as 20 in November 1771, but it is probably correct. The *Gentleman's Magazine* lists him as lately dead in April 1813 'in his 65th year' and this notice apparently derives from the fuller and more precise one in the *Warwickshire Advertiser*, which begins, 'On Friday last, March 13th, 1813, died in his 65th year, the Rev. James Eyre, master of the free-school at Solihull' and which bears the initials of Samuel Parr, his distinguished friend and benefactor over many years.[4] The *DNB* is wrong, however, in attributing his education to

---

[1] This is a slightly shortened version of a paper written in collaboration with Jeremy Warburg and published in *English Studies* 39 (1958).

[2] See note 14 below.

[3] Compiled by J. A. Venn (Cambridge 1944), Pt 2, Vol. II, p. 448.

[4] Less precisely, Parr writes of him in 1801 as being 'more than 50 years old' (W. Field, *Memoirs of the Life, Writings and Opinions of the Rev. Samuel Parr, LL.D.*, London 1828, I, 423).

St Catherine's Hall, Cambridge. There is ample evidence, including that of the *Alumni Cantabrigienses* (*loc. cit.*), to show that he was primarily an Oxford man. He matriculated, a member of Trinity College Oxford, in 1771 and proceeded to his bachelor's degree in 1775; he became a deacon in Oxford the same year and was ordained priest in Worcester in September 1776. He was headmaster of Solihull School from February 1782 until his death, and married Charlotte, the daughter of one of the Feoffees, Judd Harding.[5] They proceeded to have a large family and Eyre found that his income was inadequate. In 1801, Parr writes of his school appointment as having with it 'a tolerable house and an annual salary of 80 *l.*', to which he added a further £60 through his holding two widely separated curacies. At this time six of his ten children had been born and life was difficult: 'during the late season of distress', continues Parr, 'he has found it very difficult to procure food and raiment for the present day', let alone provide for whatever the future might have in store.[6]

These observations by Parr were addressed to Lord Chedworth to whom Parr was appealing on behalf of his friend for the living of Winterbourne Stoke, Wiltshire, which Chedworth had offered to Parr. Eyre received the living and in the following year Chedworth spontaneously offered him in addition a living at Nettleton[7] (one, incidentally, which Parr this time wanted for himself and which came both directly and indirectly to bring a good deal of trouble onto Parr's head). It was this that occasioned Eyre's connexion with Cambridge, though by no means such as is recorded in the *DNB*. In a letter to Parr on June 1802, Lord Chedworth pointed out that for Eyre to have Nettleton in addition to Winterbourne he would have to qualify 'by becoming a Master of Arts' and he offered to advance £50 to Eyre for his expenses in this connexion.[8] The *Alumni Cantabrigienses* (*loc. cit.*) records that he was granted incorporation by virtue of his Oxford BA and was admitted to the degree of MA at Caius in 1802.[9] With the two livings and his headmastership, life must have been easier, but

[5] J. Burman, *Solihull and its School* (Solihull 1939), pp. 30 f.

[6] Field, *Memoirs* (see note 4), I, p. 424.

[7] John Johnstone, *The Works of Samuel Parr, LL.D.* (London 1828), I, p. 600.

[8] *Ibid.*, I, p. 603.

[9] Cf. also J. Venn, *Biographical History of Gonville & Caius College* (cambridge 1898), II, p. 139.

when he died in 1813 he left his family ill-provided for and once again they had reason to be grateful for the goodwill of Dr Parr, who remained a practical benefactor for the rest of his own life and remembered them also in his will. By this time, there was indeed a family tie, since Parr had in 1816 taken as his second wife Eyre's sister Mary.

But the friendship between Parr and Eyre was not felt as one-sided. Indeed the meagre products of Eyre's pen which achieved print in his own lifetime seem largely to have been occasioned in Parr's defence. His written testimony figures prominently in *A Sequel to the Printed Paper Lately Circulated in Warwickshire*,[10] in which Parr minutely records the events and exchanges connected with the sordid affair of his allegation, undoubtedly well-founded, that a brother-priest, the Rev. Mr Curtis of Birmingham, had sent him two unpleasant anonymous letters. This work is of interest in the present connexion as being a clear witness to the intimacy existing between Parr and Eyre and to the extent to which Eyre was in Parr's confidence; but it testifies also to the considerable reputation that Eyre had for scholarship, learning, and sagacity. Much later, Eyre went into print again in his friend's interests, culminating in some pages in the *Gentleman's Magazine* for February 1807.[11] At the time of Lord Chedworth's giving Eyre the Nettleton living which Parr wanted, Parr asked Chedworth for a piece of plate. It seems fairly clear that his Lordship thought the less of Parr on this account, and rumours subsequently circulated not only that Chedworth talked of it as a solicited gift but also that the Latin inscription glowing with praises of Parr on the £68 soup tureen was of Parr's own composition. Eyre now revealed that he himself, at Chedworth's request, had written the inscription and was responsible for its final state except for some modifications—unspecified—which he said Parr had suggested on reading the draft.

But such services to his friend, however admirable in intention or effect, would not alone have prompted Parr to refer to him as 'a very good scholar' whose 'application to books is extensive'.[12] It was this characteristic, however, which apparently showed in

---

[10] Pp. xii, 181, London 1792. In his set of *Critical Review* (see below) Eyre left a cutting from the *Morning Chronicle*, a letter to the editor by the offending priest's famous brother, Sir William Curtis, Alderman of the City of London.

[11] Vol. lxxvii, Pt. 1, pp. 117–20.

[12] Field, *Memoirs*, I, p. 423.

his annotating his copy of Johnson's *Dictionary* to such effect as enabled Parr to bargain with Messrs Longman for £50 to be given to Eyre's family in return for the use of it in making a revised edition.[13] As it turned out, Todd found the annotations of insufficient value to enable him to use them. He says, with what seems today unjustifiable condescension,

> one cannot but admire the indefatigable industry of the scholiast, in crowding the margins with words or sentences, intended (I should suppose in very many instances) rather for future consideration, than for decided addition. Had the same attention been paid to our old authors, the labour of Mr Eyre would have been invaluable. Probably not having access to many writers of this description, Mr Eyre availed himself of the less useful information within his reach; and bestowed acute as well as diligent investigation upon objects not always deserving it. Sometimes, though rarely, he has given a citation from a book of elder times; a citation generally admissible. The writer of a future dictionary may perhaps often betake himself to this store-house of information. What I have scrupled to adopt, may, at no distant period, demand, on increasing authority, admission into an English dictionary; and eccentrick terms, which have been employed by questionable writers to express common conceptions, may perhaps lose their novelty, or their quaintness, in sage and solemn usage.[14]

Small wonder, perhaps, that in 1828 we find a reviewer of a stereotype reprint of the last folio edition of the *Dictionary* upholding the unrevised form of the *Dictionary* and ignoring Todd's revised version: 'After all the changes that have occurred since [Johnson's] death in our literature; after philologist has been pursuing philologist over the beaten track of our language, we find, after all, that we cannot better consult our own advantage than to recur to his dictionary just as he left it to the world.'[15]

Eyre's annotations do not seem to have impressed R. G. Latham, a subsequent reviser of Johnson, much more than Todd:

[13] *Bibliotheca Parriana* (London 1827), p. 247. A note by Parr adds the information that Eyre had wanted Parr to have his copy of the Dictionary and that Messrs Longman were informed of his wish. They declined to return it to him, however, sending him instead a copy of Todd's revised version, at which Parr accounted himself well satisfied.

[14] Samuel Johnson, *A Dictionary of the English Language . . . With numerous corrections and with the addition of several thousand words . . . By H. J. Todd,* I (London 1818), Introduction p. iv.

[15] *Monthly Review,* 3rd Series, vii, p. 541.

A dictionary of Mr Eyre's, with marginal annotations, though it contains many new extracts, too often refers us either to periodicals, wherein the author is anonymous, or to some novelist equally anonymous, and even more ephemeral. There is no reason, however, why words thus indicated should not be useful; and a certain proportion of them is almost sure to be so. The floating language of the day is thus preserved; and this the worst literature best exhibits. Todd . . . thinks it possible that at no distant period some may demand admission by an increase of currency and authority. Of extracts, however, that justify such an expectation, I have found but few. The rest are, in the main, what Todd calls 'eccentric terms' by 'questionable writers', expressing 'common conceptions'. I follow his example in rejecting most of these.[16]

And along with Eyre's, Latham dismisses the annotated copies of Malone and Horne Tooke. Yet, considered even through Todd's and Latham's obvious disapproval, it would seem that Eyre did indeed leave behind a 'storehouse of information' on the current usage of his time, and the revisers' scruples—so far removed from the lexicographer's approach of more recent times—are the more to be regretted inasmuch as Eyre's copy (which, as Latham makes clear, was still in the possession of Messrs Longmans, Green and Company in the early 1860s) seems now to be lost beyond recall. At any rate, our inquiries have yielded no trace of it.

Other evidence does, however, survive of Eyre's industrious habit of annotation. There is, in the Library of University College London, a collection of *The Critical Review*, many of whose volumes bear annotations in margins and endpapers to a fairly extensive degree. Almost all the volumes bear the bookplate of Samuel Parr, but rather more than thirty in the earlier part of the collection carry also, on title page or endpaper, the signature of an apparently earlier owner, James Eyre. Several of them associate Eyre with Trinity, in four cases the college being mentioned on the title page. The *Bibliotheca Parriana* (p. 277) records a run of 143 volumes of the *CR*, from its commencement in 1756 to 1816. This latter date is no misprint, since it is consistent with the number of volumes mentioned, but it is not clear why Parr should have owned a run extending only to 1816, the year of his

[16] *A Dictionary of the English Language by R. G. Latham founded on that of Dr Samuel Johnson as edited by the Rev. H. J. Todd, M.A.* Vol. I, Pt. i (London 1866), p. lxxxvii. On Latham, see further Ch. 5 below.

marriage to Eyre's sister. No mention is made of another set, nor of annotations, nor of any volumes having belonged to Eyre. Yet the Eyre-Parr set in University College, now truncated at 1800, seems originally to have extended to the year of Eyre's death: the pre-war library catalogue shows that the College once possessed the unbroken run down to 1813, and it appears that the volumes from 1801 to 1813 were destroyed by the fire-bombs of 1940. True, it is not certain how many of the volumes actually belonged to Eyre. He ceases to sign them after 1774, but annotations continue in what is almost certainly his writing until 1785—though their paucity from 1779 onwards makes it appear that 1785 is not a significant date from the point of view of ownership. Indeed, the fact that the run extended to 1813, the year of his death, would suggest that the whole of it was his own and that it came into Parr's possession after his friend's death.

There are almost 2,000 annotations altogether, fairly evenly spread over Volumes 1 to 46 but especially frequent in Volumes 37 to 45. In content, they fall into three broad classes, again fairly evenly divided numerically: miscellaneous comments, linguistic or stylistic criticisms, and ascriptions. In addition there are some scores of initial letters (J. E. P. and others), the significance of which is not at present clear.

The miscellaneous comments may be briefly exemplified. Often they are lengthy extracts from contemporary books and periodicals (the *Gentleman's Magazine* and the *Monthly Review* figure prominently). In 25/71 we find his caustic 'Ludicrous' condemning the lines ' . . . Next a form arose, / So hideous, that the sisters on their toes / Stood . . .'. He endorses the *Monthly Review*'s criticism of *Love Elegies* (10/245) to the effect that 'their dismal writer is much more in love with one Rosa, than the Muses are with him'. In 13/267, below a review of *The Musical Lady*, he notes that 'Miss Pope's admirable performance of Sophia contributed no little to the success of this pleasing Farce'.

Of the linguistic items, not many, proportionately, are concerned with lexical points, but several of those which are give us perhaps some indication of what has been lost with the annotated *Dictionary*. Authorities (and sometimes quotations) are given for a good many words and senses and these sometimes show complete independence from, and advance over, the material in Johnson. Thus Eyre is able to refute the statement (21/12) that *addicted to* implies 'a vicious pursuit' and this end is also served by his quotations from Blair, Hurd and Warton in 45/43. One might also mention that authorities are cited for *unsuppressible* (4/319), and, perhaps, for *presumable* (12/181). It is possible that these were entered in the CR from his annotated *Dictionary*, since there is abundant evidence that he resorted primarily to Johnson when he was exercised to comment on lexical matters. On a critic's objection to the phrase *good success*, for instance, he notes: 'If success be the termination of any affair happy or unhappy, how is good an improper epithet?' (10/374), which is an echo of Johnson's first definition of *success*.

But most of the linguistic points concern grammar and provide admirably full material on the typical late eighteenth-century assimilation of the prescriptive precepts laid down by standard grammarians of the time like Lowth and Ash. Practically all the points that he feels so strongly about as repeatedly to suggest preferred variants for them are precisely the stock points at issue in the grammars of the time. *You was* is changed to *you were* (e.g. 3/257, 25/55), *thou wert* to *thou wast* (e.g. 6/88, 39/130), the preterites *forbid* and *begun* to *forbad* (3/354) and *began* (35/115, 39/87); the past participles *drank, broke, swore, drove, rose, wrote, shook* are altered to the forms which have since become standard, though he alters *with-held* to the more archaic *with-holden* (39/377, 40/332). Further points which reflect his assimilation of contemporary grammars are his alterations of oblique to subject forms (e.g. 'than him' to 'than he' 3/393), 'averse to' to 'averse from' (e.g. 40/46) and 'by this means' to 'by this mean' (e.g. 39/347). He wants to see the analogy of *myself* adopted (alterations to 'hisself', e.g. 1/539, 'theirselves' e.g. 3/430) but this would not seem to represent his own natural usage (he alters 'himself' to 'themselves', 22/422). He is less in step with the precepts of his authorities in frequently altering 'mistaken' to 'mistaking' in phrases like 'we are mistaken' (e.g. 6/145) and even as an adjective ('the mistaken notions' is altered in 38/383, and similar examples occur in 29/112 and elsewhere); his own usage in this respect is illustrated by his ' . . . are certainly mistaking . . .' which occurs in a comment, 18/370.

He is severe with writers who use *will* and *would* in the first person (39/5, 37/205, 38/245; 'Will! Downright Irish! I will be drowned; nobody shall help me' is his protest in 6/62). He is untroubled by apparent inconsistency in dutifully altering 'I had rather' to 'I would rather' (39/287, 40/146). Relative clauses frequently invite his criticism ('dispute it is not our business to enter into' 3/439, 'in the state which it was taken' 36/374, 'the hour he had received it' 41/40—and many others—are altered to have a preposition followed by *which*), and he notices particularly 'from whence' which he alters to 'from which' (e.g. 22/13), though he is capable of the tautology himself, altering 'we cannot . . . say who this defender is' to 'we cannot . . . say from whence this defence proceeds' (18/399). As he observes elsewhere, 'Good use' is 'not always uniform in her decisions' (42/113).

Finally, the ascriptions: virtually all relate to the authors of works reviewed. For example, to the review of *The New Bath Guide*, Eyre adds 'By C. Anstey' (21/369); to that of *Solyman and Almena*, 'By J. Langhorne, A.M.' (13/148). He attributes *An Apology for the Life and Writings of David Hume* to 'C. Melmoth' (43/320) which is the pseudonym of Samuel Jackson Pratt to whom this work is attributed by the *Dictionary of Anonymous and Pseudonymous English Literature* of Halkett and Laing. Some uncertainty is shown over *A Gentleman's Tour through Monmouthshire and Wales* (39/358): first 'Wyndham' has been entered; this is deleted and followed by 'Mr Wynne, Salisbury'; 'Wynne' has then been deleted and the name 'Penruddock' written in the margin. Halkett and Laing attribute the work to Henry Penruddock Wyndham, and give their source of information as 'a later edition (Salisbury, 1781)'. Sometimes the ascription is wholly at variance with that given in Halkett and Laing; for example, *Sentimental Fables. Designed chiefly for the Use of the Ladies* is ascribed to Thomas Marryot in the *Dictionary* but to 'Bickerstaff' by Eyre (37/140); *An Epistle from Oberea* is ascribed to Major John Scott in the *Dictionary* but to 'Anstey' by Eyre (37/62). He makes several accepted ascriptions to Kenrick; when, therefore, to the reviews of *Lexiphanes* (23/264) and *The Sale of Authors* (24/45) he appends Kenrick's name, it is not clear whether he is attributing to Kenrick the authorship of the books or that of their reviews. *Lexiphanes* is well known to be the work of Campbell, and Halkett and Laing attribute to Campbell also *The Sale of Authors* on the authority of Prior's *Life of Malone*.

It is of course on the authorship of reviews in the *CR* that fresh knowledge is most needed. Study of this periodical 'is difficult in the absence of a marked set such as we have for the *Monthly*,[17] and scholars have regretted the loss of two known marked sets.[18] This loss may be somewhat offset by a number of ascriptions in the University College set of the *CR* which in some cases undoubtedly refer to the authors of reviews and in other cases may well do so. For example, he attributes to Smollett (6/453, the volume for 1758) the review of Kenrick's *Epistles philosophical and moral*. It is well known that Smollett reviewed for the *CR* between 1756 and about 1762, during which time he was serving as editor; in fact 'for the first five years of the journal's existence he must have been a major contributor'.[19] Those reviews which are said by Jones[20] to have been ascribed to Smollett do not include the one marked by Eyre. Eyre also attributes (56/45) the review of Blair's *Lectures on Rhetoric and Belles Lettres* to Joseph Robertson: 'This article was written by the Revd. Joseph Robertson, who . . . wrote for this Review (above 2620 articles) from 1764 to 1785.' This seems to echo the memoir written by Robertson himself and published shortly after his death in the *Gentleman's Magazine*: ' . . . he was concerned in writing the Critical Review "for twenty-one years, from August 1764, to September 1785, inclusive.["] During this period he was the author of above 2620 articles, on theological, classical, poetical, and miscellaneous publications' (lxxii, Feb. 1802, p. 110).[21]

[17] Cf. L. Landa, *English Literature 1660–1800: A Bibliography* (Princeton 1952), II, p. 863.

[18] See note 21 below.

[19] C. Jones, *Smollett Studies* (Berkeley, Calif. 1942), p. 90.

[20] *Modern Language Notes* 61 (1946), p. 440.

[21] Jones, *Smollett Studies*, p. 438, points out that a set of the *CR* in which Robertson had marked his own articles, like another marked at Archibald Hamilton's direction, has disappeared. The only review that has been definitely ascribed to Robertson is that of Bowyer's *Dissertation upon the Epistles of Phalaris . . . By Richard Bentley, D.D.*, in *CR* 43/1–12.

3

Shakespeare and the English Language

In this chapter[1] we shall be concerned chiefly with attempting to establish the kind of language study that is most significant for students of Shakespeare. The title seeks to dissociate itself on the one hand from the 'language of Shakespeare's time' (which might concern contemporary archives of a remote area having no necessary connexion with Shakespeare), and equally on the other hand from the 'language of Shakespeare' (which too often seems to imply that the poet is a sort of linguistic island). It should be superfluous to point out that the language of Shakespeare is an amalgam of the language that Shakespeare found around him— together with what he made of it. And these need to be painstakingly separated for the intelligent appraisal of Shakespeare to an extent that is quite unnecessary for the intelligent appraisal of Yeats or Eliot or Pinter.

In other words, over and above the dense complexities that must have been difficult for the Elizabethans too, there are for us in reading Shakespeare difficulties that did not exist in Shakespeare's own time. These are paradoxically aggravated by our very familiarity with the plays: as witness our 'institutionalizing' some expressions in a usage as foreign to Shakespeare as Spenser's *derring do(e)* was to Chaucer. When Iago pretends to relieve Othello's feelings with the assurance that Cassio had spoken his passionate words to Desdemona only in his sleep, Othello says 'But this denoted a foregone conclusion' (III, iii, 432) and however carefully we have studied Elizabethan English, it is very hard for us to remember in the theatre that this does not mean what we have since taken the phrase *foregone conclusion* to mean.

[1] Reprinted with minor alterations from *A New Companion to Shakespeare Studies*, ed. K. Muir and S. Schoenbaum (Cambridge 1971).

And Iago goes on, ' 'Tis a shrewd doubt, though it be but a dream', using *shrewd* in the sense 'grave, serious' which is now archaic.

The extent to which we love Shakespeare (as we love the Authorized Version) for the familiar but exalted language is a measure of our inability to respond to Shakespeare as his contemporaries did. We miss the chance of sharing an Elizabethan audience's savouring of old and new, slang and formal, pompous or fashionable, hackneyed or daring: the chance therefore of achieving the shock of pleasure comparable with what is possible for us in hearing, say, *Under Milk Wood*. But not only that: we are actually in danger of not grasping what is said. Let us remember, for example, that in the very frequent wordplay, it is often the case that one of the meanings is dead and hence, for us, no wordplay at all: Leontes' words to his little son (*The Winter's Tale* 1, ii, 123), 'We must be neat—not neat, but cleanly', will illustrate this; he replaces *neat* because of its bovine sense which suggests horns and hence cuckoldry.

It is necessary, therefore, to study the language of Shakespeare's time and then to distinguish Shakespeare's language within it. But even this is to proceed too fast. There is an important consideration which must occupy us between these two, and that is Shakespeare's interest in and reaction to the language around him: narrowly, his interest in the linguistic fashions and controversies of his time, and more broadly, his interest in the nature of language itself. What we need is thus a study involving a threefold distinction:

(1) English as it was about 1600
(2) Shakespeare's interest in his language
(3) Shakespeare's unique use of English

In speaking of Shakespeare's 'unique' use of English, it will be realized that one is speaking in linguistic terms and not in bardolatry. Every individual has a unique *parole*, a unique realization of what is possible in the language of his time and place. But at the same time this is not to deny that the *parole* of some individuals is more interesting than that of others: William Shakespeare's than Nahum Tate's, for example.

Now the language of any period can be considered as comprising three aspects: *vocabulary*—the word-stock; *grammar*—the organization of vocabulary into sentences; and thirdly *transmission*—the means of transmitting language from one person to another, either directly by the sounds of speech or indirectly by the marks of written representation.

In many respects the English of 1600 has remained unchanged in all three aspects. Many words sound the same, and are spelt the same; many grammatical patterns have remained unchanged; many words have stayed in use and in the same use, that is, with the same meaning. Our reason for studying the language of 1600, however, is that in many respects the language has changed quite sharply, and we are confronted by two difficulties. The first is the discipline of recognizing these differences. The second is the much more acute difficulty of deciding whether these differences are purely those between our time and 1600 (features which would not seem striking to Shakespeare's audience) or whether they are differences which result from Shakespeare's creativeness (and which would therefore seem individual in his own time).

So far as transmission is concerned, the complications are both less and more troublesome. Less because—*pace* those critics who have written about individual poets' 'voices'—it is doubtful whether much can be done to distinguish an author's pronunciation—still less *voice quality*—from that of his time in general. Here is one area, in fact, where confusion has been perpetuated through such terms as 'Shakespeare's pronunciation'—even used as the title of a well-known book—where little attempt is made to distinguish Shakespeare from his time and and where mainly the latter is meant. In addition, these problems are less troublesome, one might suggest, because it is equally doubtful whether a great deal is to be gained from a closer knowledge of transmission differences. Now that we have the technical ability to put on a play in roughly the pronunciation of 1600, the desirability of so doing has become less apparent. Since so many of the features of Elizabethan pronunciation have remained in twentieth-century use with utterly different sociological connotations, it is exceedingly difficult to avoid farcical overtones in ways that do not arise with original versions in French or German, or even in Chaucerian English.

The complications are *more* troublesome inasmuch as the two modes of transmission—sound and spelling—are necessarily confounded in dealing with an earlier time where the language is

couched (as to substance) in only one of these. And while both
spellings and sounds have changed, they have not changed in the
same ways and we obviously cannot infer the sound changes
from the spelling ones. Editing and interpretative scholarship
have gained (and undoubtedly can continue to gain) from the
close study of both aspects of transmission. We would rarely
think of accepting an emendation today without close reference
to the ways in which a given word was spelt in 1600 and the ways
in which that spelling could have given rise—whether from manuscript or from print—to the corruption that we suspect. And the
study of the sounds, despite the spellings, has led to a far fuller
knowledge—particularly of word-play: 'I am here', says Touchstone to the bucolic Audrey, 'I am here with thee and thy goats,
as the most capricious poet, honest Ovid, was among the Goths'
(*As You Like It* III, iii, 4). The connexion between *goats* and
capricious on the one hand and *Goths* on the other is obscured alike
by Elizabethan spelling, our own spelling, and our modern
pronunciation. It is only when we know that the pronunciation of
Goth was different in Shakespeare's time that the full connexion,
the full range of the pun, can become apparent. Spelling and
modern pronunciation disguise a pun similarly in Hotspur's
'That roan shall be my throne' (*1 Henry IV* II, iii, 67).[2]

To turn now to grammar, we find here very great and significant differences from the habits of our own time, but at least we
are helped by the fact that they are for the most part obvious to us.
They are not obscured by spelling as in transmission or by continuity of form as with vocabulary. Not usually, at any rate but
there are snares here too, even in so seemingly innocent a form as
his. In *Hamlet*, III, iii, the King's soliloquy presents him considering the relative ease with which justice can be evaded in 'the
corrupted currents of this world'. But, he goes on (60–62),

> 'tis not so above:
> There is no shuffling; there the action lies
> In his true nature.

During the summer of 1966, at the Stratford production by Peter
Hall, I heard the player heavily emphasize *his*, apparently under

---

[2] Cf. H. Kökeritz, *Shakespeare's Pronunciation* (New Haven 1953), pp.
320 f., E. J. Dobson, *English Pronunciation 1500–1700*, 2nd edn (Oxford 1968),
p. 1010.

the impression (and certainly conveying the impression to the audience) that the reference was to God's nature, thus convicting Shakespeare at once of woolly expression and bad theology, if not of actual nonsense. Yet *his* as the genitive of *it* (here referring to *action*) was a contemporary commonplace, however much the salt has subsequently lost his savour. E. A. Abbott dismisses the point as too well-known to merit more than a single line, though he spends a page examining exceptions such as *its* and *it*.

Scarcely less firmly 'trodden under foot of men' is our former awareness of another pronominal usage, the distinction between *you* and *thou*, though many studies have been published on this point.[3] Even when we are intellectually aware of the distinction, however, it is hard to school ourselves to the appropriate reaction when we are in the theatre, and in any case there remain misconceptions among scholars themselves. It is often said that the old singular and plural are used in Shakespeare as they are used in Chaucer: and this is quite untrue. It is often said that in 1600 *you* was polite, formal usage but *thou* was familiar or insulting. This is a gross oversimplification. The modern linguistic concept of contrast operating through *marked* and *unmarked* members can give us a truer picture. *You* is usually the stylistically unmarked form: it is not so much 'polite' as 'not impolite'; it is not so much 'formal' as 'not informal'.

It is for this reason that *thou* can operate in such a wide variety of contrasts with *you*. At one extreme we have the solemnity and formality of religious discourses as in Edmund's 'Thou, Nature, art my goddess; to thy law My services are bound' (*King Lear* I, ii, 1 f.). Then again we have the very antonym of this in pure contempt: there is Sir Toby's advice to Sir Andrew Aguecheek in drafting the challenge to his rival, 'Taunt him with the license of ink; if thou thou'st him some thrice, it shall not be amiss' (*Twelfth Night* III, ii, 40 f.). But we need to notice that in this instance the device draws attention to the fact that while Andrew and Fabian are using the unmarked *you* to each other and to Sir Toby, Sir Toby is using *thou* to Sir Andrew with more than a suggestion of the contempt he is advising Sir Andrew to use with the count's

---

[3] Notably, T. Finkenstaedt, *You und Thou: Studien zur Anrede im Englischen* (Berlin 1963), A. McIntosh, '*As You Like It*: A Grammatical Clue to Character', *Rev. of Eng. Lit.* 4 (1963), J. Mulholland, '*Thou* and *You* in Shakespeare', *English Studies* 48 (1967).

serving man. It is essential to realize that it is not Sir Toby's use of *thou* as such which conveys his lack of respect; it is the fact that he is doing so in a social context which makes it appropriate for other speakers to use *you*. If we compare the exchanges between Falstaff and Prince Hal in *1 Henry IV*, we see sharply different values given to *thou* because the contrasts in which it operates are different. Both pass back and forth between the unmarked *you* and the marked *thou* of anger or intimacy: but there is no distancing between them in the pronoun usage and so no social opposition enters the situation. At a given moment both are using either *you* (as in Hal's 'How now, woolsack! What mutter you?' and Falstaff's 'You Prince of Wales! . . . Are you not a coward?' II, iv, 127 ff.) or else, as a little later in the same scene, they are both using *thou* (Falstaff's 'Dost thou hear me, Hal?' and the Prince's 'Ay, and mark thee too, Jack', *ibid.* 202).

The significance of the active contrast between *you* and *thou* is brought out excellently in the first scene of *King Lear*. Kent, Gloucester, Edmund and Lear all use *you* in speaking to each other: as we should expect. Goneril, Regan and Cordelia address their father as *you*—again as we should expect. Lear addresses Goneril and Regan as *thou*, and again—from father to daughter— this is what we should expect. Against this background of perfect decorum and the fully expected, it should no doubt come as a surprise to us that Lear addresses Cordelia at first as *you*: 'what can you say to draw/A third more opulent than your sisters?' (I, i, 84 f.). So also 93 f. It seems unlikely that these uses of *you(r)* are without significance in indicating a special feeling that Lear has for the girl he calls 'our joy', who has been, as France says, Lear's 'best object', the argument of his praise, the balm of his age, the best, the dearest (*ibid.* 214–16). When, however, he is shocked by what he takes to be her lack of love, he uses *thou*—not now the *thou* of father to daughter but the *thou* of anger: 'But goes thy heart with this?' 'Thy truth, then, be thy dower!' (104, 107). This is what is meant by saying the importance lies in *active contrast*. Although *you* is the general unmarked form beside which the use of *thou* is conspicuous, the position is that in a relationship where *thou* is expected, *you* can likewise be in contrast and conspicuous. This becomes apparent again and again in the scenes that follow: Lear grows cool to Goneril and the change is reflected in the use of *you*: 'Are you our daughter?' 'Your name, fair gentlewoman?'

(I, iv, 218, 235), and he turns to Regan with his customary affectionate paternal *thou* for these two daughters: 'Beloved Regan, Thy sister's naught' (II, iv, 131 f.). The Fool addresses the disguised Kent as *you*; Regan conspiring with Goneril's steward expresses her ultimate acknowledgement of their partnership by coming down the intimacy scale from *you* to *thou*: 'So fare you well . . . Fare thee well' (IV, v, 36, 40).

If it is only with difficulty that we today can respond to this contrast of *you* and *thou*, our sensitivity is still less in relation to the use of the second person pronoun with imperatives. The pronoun may have subject form or object form or it may be absent, and in some cases—17, according to a recent study[4]—all three possibilities can occur with the same verb:

Come thou on my side.	(*Richard III* I, iv, 263)
Come thee on.	(*Antony and Cleopatra* IV, vii, 16)
Come on my right hand.	(*Julius Caesar* I, ii, 213)

While it would be idle to pretend that these three forms of imperative were always carefully distinguished in meaning at this time, we must not assume that they were usually synonymous. Leaving out of account reflexive use like *calm thee*, it would seem that, beside an 'unmarked' imperative without any pronoun, the form with *thou* was emphatic; this is frequently clear from the metre or the context, as when the Second Murderer refuses to profit from the death of Clarence:

> Take thou the fee, and tell him what I say.
> (*Richard III* I, iv, 275)

The pronoun subject becomes especially contrastive when the *do* auxiliary is also used, as when Queen Margaret begs for death:

> What, wilt thou not? Then, Clarence, do it thou.
> . . . sweet Clarence, do thou do it.
> (*3 Henry VI* v, v, 71, 73)

Or, in a different vein, Falstaff's plea:

> Do not thou, when thou art king, hang a thief.
> (*1 Henry IV* I, ii, 60)

[4] C. Millward, 'Pronominal Case in Shakespearian Imperatives', *Language* 42 (1966).

On the other hand, the imperative with the objective form of the pronoun (which may be better explained as an unstressed form of the subject pronoun) seems rather to seek the personal involvement of the addressee. We may compare Polonius' farewell to his son:

> Farewell; my blessing season this in thee!
>
> *(Hamlet* I, iii, 81)

with the Ghost's to his son:

> Fare thee well at once . . .
> Adieu, adieu, adieu! Remember me.
>
> *(Ibid.* v, 88, 91)

It is naturally especially common with verbs used to summon attention, such as *look* and *hark*: for example,

> But hear thee, Gratiano:
> Thou art too wild. . . .
>
> *(The Merchant of Venice* II, ii, 165 f.)

Mention has been made of the *do* auxiliary. Shakespeare witnessed the increasing association of this auxiliary with questions, negation, and emphasis (*Do you go? I don't go, I DO go*), but for the most part a choice remained which could be used for stylistic contrast. As Mrs. Salmon has pointed out,[5] Jacques Bellot was among Shakespeare's contemporaries one of those most plainly aware of the use of *do* to confer a weighty and sonorous rotundity, observing that people 'doe adde commonly the verb Faire, before the other verbes, for the replenishing and sounding of their tongue with more grace' (*Le Maistre d'Escole Anglais*). It is in this knowledge that we must savour Falstaff's coloured rhetoric when he plays the King:

> This pitch, as ancient writers do report, doth defile.
>
> *(I Henry IV* II, iv, 400)

or when he exults in Mistress Page's passion for him:

> O, she did so course o'er my exteriors with such a greedy intention that the appetite of her eye did seem to scorch me up like a burning-glass.
>
> *(The Merry Wives of Windsor* I, iii, 62 ff.)

[5] V. Salmon, 'Sentence Structures in Colloquial Shakespearian English', *Trans. Phil. Soc.* (1965).

The purpose has been to show that even the minutiae of grammar present significant differences in Elizabethan English; it goes without saying that such differences are no less relevant in larger matters such as clause and sentence structure. But it is time we glanced at the remaining aspect of language, vocabulary. The difficulties here—as in transmission—are often disguised. That is to say, we really do not come upon many entirely strange words in Shakespeare that hoist a danger signal warning us to consult Onions[6] or the *OED*. When Salerio in *The Merchant of Venice* says 'Slubber not business for my sake' (ii, viii, 39), we are compelled to look up *slubber* ('treat carelessly'). Later in the play, Portia says that she speaks too long, 'to peize the time' (iii, ii, 22), meaning to weigh it down and make it slow. The problem of entirely strange words is not, of course, to be underrated, and there are plenty in Shakespeare 'stranger' than *slubber* and *peize*: *chopine* (a kind of shoe) and *eisel* (vinegar) occur in *Hamlet*, *kecksy* (a wild plant) and *sutler* (camp-follower) in *Henry V*. And generations of editors, let alone readers, have been puzzled by Petruchio's

> Sit down, Kate, and welcome. Soud, soud, soud, soud.
> *(The Taming of the Shrew* iv, i, 125)

Many have taken it to be a nonsense-word, part of the snatch of song that has just preceded, or an exclamation; some have preferred to emend *s* to *f*. This is a good illustration of the great scope still remaining for work on Shakespeare's problem words and Dr Hulme has argued in favour of reading *u* as *n*, the word *sonde* in the sense of 'food' having been certainly still current in the mid-fifteenth century.[7]

But the problem of overtly strange words is less than the problem of words which disguise their strangeness. We meet a large number of words more or less familiar in their graphic substance, but with different meanings which we can easily ignore, to our loss, since very frequently the modern meaning will make some kind of sense in the Shakespearian context. For example, Polonius tells Reynaldo to 'breathe' his son's faults 'quaintly' (*Hamlet* ii, i, 31) and we may link Polonius with quaintness in the modern sense without surprise; but Polonius means the insinuation to be

---

[6] C. T. Onions, *A Shakespeare Glossary*, 2nd edn (Oxford 1919).
[7] H. M. Hulme, *Explorations in Shakespeare's Language* (London 1962).

done *artfully*. Iago's *shrewd doubt* quoted earlier would also make sense in terms of the present-day meanings, but we are the losers if we do not realise that *shrewd* means 'serious'. We are still further misled if we do not understand Edmund's 'pretence of danger' in its Elizabethan sense, 'dangerous or malicious purpose' (*King Lear* I, ii, 84). Similar examples will spring to mind: *important* often meant 'importunate', *perfection* 'performance'; *humour*, *frank*, *kind*, *husband*, *sad*, *safe*, *quick*, *respect*—one could make a very long list of words which are among the commonest today but whose modern meaning is, as C. S. Lewis categorized it, the 'dangerous' one when we meet them as common words also in Shakespeare.[8]

All these differences—in transmission, grammar, and vocabulary—are part of the normal linguistic process. Similar differences can be found in comparing the language of Chaucer or of Dr Johnson with our own: change is unchanging, so to say; only the examples of linguistic change differ from comparison to comparison. But each age has its special linguistic preoccupations too: in Chaucer's time, for instance, the co-existence with a largely popular English of a largely courtly French; in Dr Johnson's the problem of reducing the language to teachable rule in the light of enlightenment and rationalism, and in the face of a growing middle class that was literate. In Shakespeare's time, too, there were special preoccupations—the post-Renaissance experimentation with language, a fluidity of linguistic fashion and a new literary self-consciousness on the part of writers in the vernacular; an ambition to achieve a literature in English to match that of the classical languages or at any rate that of French or Italian.

I have just used the word *fluidity*, but we must be cautious here. I applied it to linguistic fashion, not to the language itself. Again and again, one finds writers on Shakespeare's language describing a ruleless norm-less flux—a bright chaotic galaxy only constellated by the bard's genius, who created patterns that were entirely original and *sui generis*. We all know this to be wholly distorted, but despite our intellectual awareness of this, its effect as a piece of critical rhetoric (not to say folklore) on our imagination seems unavoidable from time to time. All languages (we must continually remind ourselves) are always in a state of flux. And when we consider the linguistic originality with which English has been

[8] C. S. Lewis, *Studies in Words* (Cambridge 1968).

used in the past eighty years by men like Hopkins, Joyce, or even Dylan Thomas, we must see that the artist of our own time is no more restricted by a rule-ful, norm-ful language than Shakespeare was. The ways in which Shakespeare is seen as being defiantly independent often (if not usually) concern word-formation and in particular 'conversion' from one part of speech to another: but of course this is a property of English in all periods not merely of Shakespeare's period, still less of Shakespeare alone. Again, only specific examples of the process are Shakespeare's.

'Chaos and fire-new, unharnessed energy.' 'A buccaneering spirit in language as well as on the high seas.' Gross, romantic distortions? Not entirely, we must admit. There was less *sense of fixity* about the language in 1600 than in some other periods, and also more outspoken controversy and overt interest in the medium. The cult of the hard word as a necessity and indeed a virtue is something which runs through the whole period. *Ovids Banquet of Sence* (1595) shows Chapman delighting in obscure new words and elegant conceits; *disparent* seemingly used by no one else, appears on the second page. He says in his preface:

> that Poesie should be as perviall as Oratorie, and plainnes her speciall ornament, were the plaine way to barbarisme . . . it serves not a skilfull Painters turne, to draw the figure of a face onely to make knowne who it represents; but hee must lymn, give luster, shaddow, and heightning; which though ignorants will esteeme spic'd, and too curious, yet such as have the judiciall perspective, will see it hath motion, spirit, and life. . . . Obscuritie in affection of words, and indigested concets, is pedanticall and childish; but where it shroudeth it selfe in the hart of his subiect, uttered with fitnes of figure, and expressive Epethites; with that darknes wil I still labour to be shaddowed; rich Minerals are digd out of the bowels of the earth, not found in the superficies and dust of it.

In 1595 we have the fashion for augmenting the language as it flourished with Thomas Elyot, the counter-movement against excess augmentation from the inkhorn as fought by Thomas Wilson and Puttenham, and now with Chapman and others the rejoinder that, yes, *affected* and *pedantic* obscurities for their own sake are to be repudiated, but a high degree of ornamentation and precision is required and to this end 'rich Minerals' must continue to be 'digd out of the bowels of the earth'.

One needs to stress this tug of war because it is commonly said that Shakespeare scorned the inkhorn, and one can cite many passages which seem to support this. 'I have receiv'd my proportion, like the Prodigious Son', says Launce in *The Two Gentlemen of Verona* (II, iii, 3) and as Silvia says in the following scene (line 30), 'A fine volley of words' can be 'quickly shot off'. Shakespeare is aware that the unlearned can be injudiciously attracted by high-sounding language with his Hostess Quickly's *honeysuckle* for 'homicidal', *honey-seed* for 'homicide' (*2 Henry IV* II, i, 47 f.), his Dogberry and Verges, and his Costard ('welcome the sour cup of prosperity! Affliction may one day smile again': *Love's Labour's Lost* I, i, 291). Launcelot's *impertinent* (*The Merchant of Venice* II, ii, 124) confuses 'pertinent' and 'important' in its contemporary sense of 'urgent'. Benvolio mocks the Nurse by using *indite* for *invite* (*Romeo and Juliet* II, iv, 125), a malapropism elsewhere used by Hostess Quickly (*2 Henry IV* II, i, 25).

But this is not to scorn augmentation and the inkhorn: there was no disagreement on this point—that the uneducated would make ridiculous errors. John Hart, the Chester Herald, had pointed this out in his *Methode* of 1570, when he gave examples such as *temporal* for 'temperate', *certisfied* for both 'certified' and 'satisfied', *dispense* for 'suspense'. It was an undoubted fact, to which George Baker had testified in 1576 (*The New Jewel of Health*), that some people, 'more curious than wyse, esteeme of nothing but that which is most rare, or in harde and unknowne languages', and we recall Don Adriano de Armado and his 'posteriors of this day', which 'the rude multitude call the afternoon' and which is an expression that seems to Holofernes 'liable, congruent, and measurable' (*Love's Labour's Lost* v, i, 76–8). Again, there was no disagreement on this: as in the passage quoted from Chapman above, the use of learned language for obscurity's sake was ridiculous and Shakespeare shows it to be so, just as he shows the ignorant *attempt* at learned language to be so. From Armado to Polonius and beyond, we have characters who draw out the thread of their verbosity finer than the staple of their argument, as Holofernes puts it (*Love's Labour's Lost* v, i, 14), and it is not only he and Nathaniel who are laughed at for having 'been at a great feast of languages and stol'n the scraps' (*ibid.* 34).

Nathaniel may speak of abrogating scurrility (*Love's Labour's Lost* IV, ii, 51), Touchstone of abandoning the society of this female, 'which in the boorish' is leave the company of this woman (*As You Like It* v, i, 42 ff.), and this is ridiculous. But when Macbeth likewise pairs a learned expression with its 'boorish' equivalent as in

> this my hand will rather
> The multitudinous seas incarnadine,
> Making the green one red
>
> (II, ii, 61–3)

or earlier:

> If th' assassination
> Could trammel up the consequence, and catch,
> With his surcease, success; that but this blow
> Might be the be-all and the end-all here
>
> (I, vii, 2–5)

he is not being ridiculous. Here is the inkhorn used in deadly earnest, deliberately, as an expressive virtue. And this is the position taken up, as we saw, by Chapman and this was even the ultimate position of Cheke and Wilson: augmentation was necessary, the language was deficient in aureate expression. A generation before Shakespeare was born, Skelton was pointing out that the language was so 'rude' and lacking in 'pollysshed tearmes'

> That if I wold apply
> To write ornatly
> I wot not where to finde
> Tearmes to serve my mynde.

As poets felt particularly acutely the language's need, so it was they who supplied the need most discriminatingly. Puttenham (*The Arte of English Poesie*, 1589) acknowledges the services that poets have rendered in 'their studious endevours, commendably employed in enriching and polishing their native Tongue'. Nash (*Pierce Penilesse*, 1592) praises 'the Poets of our time' for having 'cleansed our language from barbarisme' and Gervase Markham (*The Gentlemans Academie*, 1595) praises them for having given English its new 'glory and exact compendiousness'. Francis Meres lists Shakespeare and Chapman among the poets by whom 'the English tongue is mightily enriched, and gorgeouslie invested in rare ornaments and resplendent abiliments', and speaks specifically of 'Shakespeares fine filed phrase' (*Palladis Tamia*, 1598).

While Shakespeare laughed at the excesses of augmentation, therefore, he was himself deeply engaged in the process and was acknowledged to be so. He was similarly ambivalent about euphuism. There is the burlesque of Launce and Speed in *The Two Gentlemen of Verona* (for example, III, i) or of Osric (*Hamlet* v, ii). There is Falstaff: 'for though the camomile, the more it is trodden on the faster it grows, yet youth, the more it is wasted the sooner it wears' (*1 Henry IV* II, iv, 388). Yet the forced ingenuity of symmetry and image characteristic of euphuist prose can be detected in serious verse too: in *Richard III*, in *Othello*, not least in *1 Henry IV*. Two scenes after Falstaff's burlesque, we have the King speaking somewhat in the ridiculed vein:

> whereof a little
> More than a little is by much too much.
> So, when he had occasion to be seen,
> He was but as the cuckoo is in June,
> Heard, not regarded, seen, but with such eyes
> As, sick and blunted with community,
> Afford no extraordinary gaze,
> Such as is bent on sun-like majesty.
>
> (III, ii, 72–9)

One final facet of linguistic fashion deserves a mention. Robert Cawdrey's *Table Alphabeticall* of 1604 echoes the well-known condemnation by Thomas Wilson fifty years earlier of those who 'pouder their talke with oversea language'. The fashion has been sustained over half a century whereby 'He that commeth lately out of Fraunce, will talke French English. . . . An other chops in with English Italienated.' Indeed, said Wilson, 'I dare sweare this, if some of their mothers were alive, thei were not able to tell what they say' (*Arte of Rhetorique*, 1553). 'The pox of such antic, lisping, affecting fantasticoes; these new tuners of accent', says Mercutio; 'these fashion-mongers, these pardon me's' (*Romeo and Juliet* II, iv, 27, 32).

Small wonder, then, if engaged so deeply in the linguistic foibles, fashions, controversies, and creativeness of his time, that Shakespeare's interest should extend also to the scepticism about the linguistic sign itself which was current if far from dominant in Elizabethan and Jacobean thought. Every man's language 'is eloquent ynough for hym self', writes a translator of Peter Ramus in 1574, countering the argument of the superiority of Latin, 'and that of others in respect of it is had as barbarous'. 'That which we call a rose By any other name would smell as sweet', and if Juliet (*Romeo and Juliet* II, ii, 43 f.) cannot claim the poet's sanction any more than Falstaff with his 'What is honour? A word' (*1 Henry IV* v, i, 132), it can be fairly claimed that they both have greater sanction than Juliet's nurse to whom primitive word-magic is attributed in 'Doth not rosemary and Romeo begin both with the same letter?' (*Romeo and Juliet* II, iv, 201).

The word-magic game is one that Cordelia refuses to play in reply to Lear's 'what can you say to draw / A third more opulent than your sisters? . . . mend your speech a little' (*King Lear* I, i, 85, 93).[9] It may seem ironical but it is no contradiction that the man who could use words to greatest effect was one who saw most clearly and sophisticatedly the distinction between 'words, words, mere words' and 'matter from the heart' (*Troilus and Cressida* v, iii, 108), and was able to frame so sardonic a speculation for Bolingbroke on the power of words:

> How long a time lies in one little word!
> Four lagging winters and four wanton springs
> End in a word: such is the breath of Kings.
> (*Richard II* I, iii, 213 ff.)

But it is time to say a few words—and space alone forbids more—on the last leg of my proposed tripos. First, the language of Shakespeare's time; second, Shakespeare's interest in the language of his time; and only then shall we, thirdly, be in a position to attempt useful observations about his own use of the language of his time.

And how many there are to make! When all is done to get things into perspective, to see the rich texture of the language in Shakespeare's time, there is still a great deal of individuality in Shakespeare's usage. In word-formation, for instance, and particularly in verb-formation. The dynamic element in Shakespeare's clauses is characteristically the most sharply pointed, and he is particularly fond of verbs with the prefixes *be-* and *en-*. Albany tells his wife 'Bemonster not thy feature' (*King Lear* IV, ii, 63),

[9] Cf. M. M. Mahood, *Shakespeare's Wordplay* (London 1957).

Kent speaks of Lear's 'unnatural and bemadding sorrow' (III, i, 38), and it is worth considering the verbal force that *bemadding* has retained here beside the comparatively static, attributive value acquired by *maddening*, which was coined later. As for verbs with *en-*, one need cite only Cassio's lines in *Othello*:

> The gutter'd rocks, and congregated sands,
> Traitors ensteep'd to enclog the guiltless keel
>
> (II, i, 69 f.)

(or, with Kenneth Muir in the Penguin edition of 1968, *enscarped* 'abruptly shelved', in place of *ensteep'd*). And highly charged verbs emerge also from the direct-conversion process: 'The hearts That spaniel'd me at heels' (still more if with some scholars we prefer *pannelled* to Hanmer's emendation) in *Antony and Cleopatra* IV, xii, 20 f., or Edgar's tightly compressed 'He childed as I father'd' (*King Lear* III, vi, 110).

Even his noun units often have a dynamic, verbal character as we see from 'gutter'd rocks, and congregated sands' just quoted from *Othello*. This is no less noticeable in many of the image-decked noun phrases in the Sonnets: 'Your own dear-pur-chas'd right (Sonnet 117), 'your ne'er-cloying sweetness' (118), 'fore-bemoaned moan' (30), 'his sweet up-locked treasure' (52), 'the time-bettering days' (82), 'proud-pied April' (98), [Time's] 'bending sickle's compass' (116). And as these complex, clause-embedding modifiers may turn our minds to Hopkins, one may also cite 'the world-without-end hour' in Sonnet 57.

Perhaps because grammatical patterning had so recently been exploited *ad nauseam* in the euphuistic style, lexical patterning may be presumed to be nearer the centre of Shakespeare's interest. We may quote from Mortimer's speech to his keepers in *1 Henry VI* to illustrate what is meant:

> Weak shoulders, overborne with burdening grief,
> And pithless arms, like to a withered vine
> That droops his sapless branches to the ground.
> Yet are these feet, whose strengthless stay is numb,
> Unable to support this lump of clay,
> Swift-winged with desire to get a grave.
>
> (II, v, 10 ff.)

Hardly the bard at his best, yet there is very considerable complexity in what he is attempting, a complexity in lexicology not syntax; or, rather, in that kind of 'lexical syntax' in which some modern linguists are becoming increasingly interested. *Weak* has a grammatical link (as modifier) with *shoulders*; *shoulders* is linked lexically to *burdening*, since there is a traditional collocation *burden—shoulder*; 'weak with grief' is thus achieved through the network of lexical and grammatical links. From *shoulders* to the lexically connected *arms*; but *arms* is grammatically linked to *pithless* which then lexically connects with *vine*, while conversely the grammatical modifier of *vine* (*withered*) works back to *arms* which become the *sapless branches* of the following line, though the direct lexical congruence is with *vine*. The *feet*, as part of a lexical series with *shoulders* and *arms*, have a grammatically-specified *stay* which is *strengthless* and *numb*; at this point we may notice the morphological as well as semantic links between *pithless*, *sapless* and *strengthless*, the first two collocating most naturally with *vine* but (especially with the help of the third) working well with the human limbs. The *stay* has both a grammatical and a lexical link with *support*, and the latter looks back to *shoulder* and *burden* lexically as well as forward to *lump of clay*, the lexical link in addition to the grammatical one working to counteract any feeling of 'mixed' metaphor. The last line, apart from a lexical connexion between *clay* and *grave*, sees a lightning antithesis to the heavily-endorsed overburdened weakness of the preceding lines, an antithesis that is Mercurial in two senses as the feet become swift-winged with desire to get a grave.

Lexical congruence working through, without, or in defiance of syntactic structure is, of course, the stock machinery of imagery, and characteristically the Shakespearian image is developed in a pairing of lexical items through syntax or collocation or both. The latter—the most straightforward—is seen, for example, in the adequacy with which Ulysses' musical image is established in the words, 'untune that string' (*Troilus and Cressida* I, iii, 109). Syntax and collocation working independently produce more complex images; we may compare with the Ulysses example the following:

> Unthread the rude eye of rebellion.
>
> (*King John* v, iv, 11)

In addition to the grammatical (verb–object) connexion between *unthread* and *eye*, there is a discontinuous lexical connexion between *eye*'s premodifier *rude* and postmodifier *rebellion*, the transverse arrangement helping to remove the danger of destroying the image by an unwelcome mixture. A somewhat similar effect can be observed in

> Heaven stops the nose at it, and the moon winks
>
> (*Othello* IV, ii, 78)

where the two clauses are grammatically related by co-ordination, by subjects that collocate (*heaven* and *moon*), and by predicates that are lexically congruent also: closing nose and eye. But it is the transverseness of these lexical links that minimizes the incongruence in the image of heaven stopping its nose. In the following example from *As You Like It* there is a discontinuous linkage with a different arrangement:

> . . . weed your better judgments
> Of all opinion that grows rank in them.
>
> (II, vii, 45 f.)

The two verbs *weed* and *grows* are lexically congruent, and to this set belongs also the complement *rank* (for *weed* and *rank*, compare *Hamlet* I, ii, 135 f.; III, iv, 151 f.). Nested between *weed* and *grows* are two nouns which likewise collocate; the fact that both are equally and analogously incongruent with the verbs to which they are grammatically linked (as object and subject respectively) helps to establish and empower an image that depends upon an 'unlexical' sequence.

But given the phenomenon of multiple meaning, a single lexical sign can self-collocate and produce the congruent collocation in more than one direction from itself. There is an example of this in Portia's well-known 'mercy' speech, the pivotal word being *strain'd* (*The Merchant of Venice* IV, i, 179), Shylock has just asked 'On what compulsion must I?' and so *strain'd* in Portia's reply has an obvious backward link to this: there is no compulsiveness in mercy. But then it works forward also to the dropping of the gentle rain: mercy is not filtered, drop by drop, from heaven. It is worth considering the *sullied–solid* crux in this light too (*Hamlet* I, ii, 129). Thus it would seem that the phonological experts can allow us a neutralized phonetic contrast.[10] At the same time the semantic span is well motivated, so that while at the point of

[10] Cf. Dobson, *English Pronunciation*, pp. 581 ff., 592 f., and notes.

utterance the word's relations are backwards to the pollution by the Queen's incest,[11] thereafter it seems perverse to ignore the lexical congruity of *solid* with the *melt* that leads to *thaw, resolve,* and *dew* in the next line.[12]

There is a more obvious 'syntactic' movement through lexical interaction when multiple meaning is allowed to emerge in the course of repetition. Leontes' reaction to *neat* may be adduced again, 'We must be neat—not neat, but cleanly' (*The Winter's Tale* i, ii, 123), in which only the first occurrence may be said to collocate with *cleanly*. But his use of *play* is a better illustration:

> Go, play, boy, play; thy mother plays, and I
> Play too; but so disgrac'd a part . . .
>
> (*Ibid.* 187 f.)

The second instance of *play* is in part colloquial repetition but it is partly also the sinister turning point, a lingering over the word which releases the sexual sense (*OED* 10c) in which the third instance occurs, indicated collocationally by the female subject; the fourth instance again shows by collocation (*part*) its ironically different use.

There are of course many aspects of Shakespeare's use of English and many approaches to his language that can sharpen and enrich our reaction to the plays and poems. It would not have been practicable here to explore more than a meagre selection of the possibilities, and equally it has not seemed appropriate to attempt a wider coverage at the expense of depth. The concentration on certain facets reflects my belief that it is especially through further study of the interrelations of grammatical and lexical patterns that linguists can in the immediate future offer contributions most readily compatible with and contributory to the insights of literary scholarship.

[11] Cf. W. H. Clemen, *The Development of Shakespeare's Imagery* (London 1951), p. 114.
[12] Cf. M. M. Mahood, *Shakespeare's Wordplay* (London 1957), pp. 16, 22.

4

The 'Language' of Language and Literature

It is probably fair to say that the current aims of teaching Old English (or 'Anglo-Saxon') and Middle English are for the most part to help students to approach the literature written before Henry V (or indeed before *Henry V*) with understanding and enjoyment. They are expected to find exercise for their critical faculty broadly (and some would say precisely) analogous to that involved in their work on post-Renaissance literature. We may need to persuade students that these aims are feasible, and—since we are realists—we also need to demonstrate the relevance to so obviously desirable a goal of the slow, exacting spadework which is bound to be resisted and resented if there is doubt or despair about the objective. These aims are by no means new but they have continued to be widely obscured and at times even denied.

There are of course formidable obstacles to speedy enjoyment of Old and Middle English literature, but perhaps most persistent is the lack of critical standards—a frustrated feeling of being rudderless in a swirl of oddly-spelled words. As a result, there has been perpetuated a dichotomy between the relatively modern writings that can be 'appreciated' (these are called 'literature') and the relatively early writings that cannot (and these are called 'language'). The distinction is unfortunate, and so is the way it is designated. It seeks, from a medievalist viewpoint, to degrade medieval writings, by not calling them 'literature'; and it has the additionally unfortunate side-effect (from a linguist's viewpoint) of degrading 'language' by equating it with what is alleged to be quaint, archaic, or dull. Self-evident as the absurdity is, it seems well-nigh impossible to eradicate the belief that language ceased when Chaucer started to use it.

It may well be natural in mother-tongue studies to regard as something rather separate a discipline showing affinities with foreign-language learning. But this can hardly be sufficient to exclude consideration of medieval writings as 'literature'. Language-learning of a far tougher order, after all, is required of those English-speaking students who seek to be interested in Camus or Brecht than of those embarking on *The Pearl* or *Beowulf*; but one does not in consequence devalue French and German literature. There must be other factors—cultural remoteness, for instance. For all their linguistic exoticness, Camus and Brecht speak in a socio-cultural ambiance that is familiar; the Middle Ages constitute a world whose structure and values are ironically more foreign—thanks to the Renaissance and the distillation of classical education—than those of Seneca or Euripides.

Another important factor is the accident determining the focus of interest in medieval writings throughout the nineteenth century. Because of the exciting discoveries in comparative philology and especially in the history of the Germanic languages on the one hand, and the application of the same 'historical method' on the other hand to *Volkskunde* and *Deutsche Mythologie*, there was little motivation for considering the medieval works simply as literature. Everything was dominated by the holy union of Gothic romanticism and historical linguistics, with the latter on the whole making the running. 'Passionless bride, divine Philology', as Tennyson almost said. In fact, however, comparative philology was scarcely passionless and she was certainly not barren. The Grimm brothers are emblematic, making profound contributions to sound law and folklore with a fine impartiality and ambidexterity. And when scholars drew back at what they considered the folkloristic and mythological excesses of men like Karl Müllenhoff and Max Müller, philology was left in sole and virtually unchallenged favour. A teacher of mine was taught by P. G. Thomas at Bedford College London in the early years of this century, and by all accounts it did not then seem inappropriate that the good professor should expound *Beowulf* solely in terms of the mixed dialectal forms manifested by the late tenth-century manuscript in which the poem comes down to us.

Language work in this very narrow sense had amply demonstrated how essential it was for the interpretation of early writings and for the establishment and necessary emendation of the texts. Contributions of this kind continued to be demanded of such work, and were readily forthcoming. Whether these have been so central or so dominating as to merit labelling the literature studied as 'language' is another matter. For one thing, philology was not the only valuable ancillary discipline for the interpretation of texts: history, archaeology, anthropology, diplomatic are among the studies that amply justified themselves by the criterion of good works. But to some extent they justified also the withholding of the honoured title of 'literature' since they conspired to keep scholars busy doing almost anything but evaluating the texts from a purely literary viewpoint. Philology and her ancillaries, it is now said, substituted commentary for criticism.

There is a great deal of substance in the charge. We now have many editions of early texts by scholars sensitive to literary values, but there is an impressive survival rate for standard editions of literature as late as Chaucer himself where introductions and notes are a miscellany of facts about phonology, dialect, variant readings, emendations, source materials, analogue allusions, and other kinds of 'background'. Especially with pre-Chaucerian texts, this is quite frequently to the total exclusion of any note conveying the editor's suggestion of the kind of response his author is trying to evoke.

Again, we now have general accounts of medieval writing where the emphasis is solidly on the works as literature. Significantly, the title of S. B. Greenfield's study of Old English literature is prefixed by the adjective *critical*.[1] But many present-day teachers of medieval literature were thoroughly imbued with a very different approach. If they were students in the 1940s, perhaps even more recently, one book they were encouraged to study as a handy and trustworthy compendium was E. E. Wardale's *Chapters on Old English Literature* (London 1935). In one northern British university in the mid-1950s this book was thought sufficiently important for there to be no less than six copies available to be borrowed by the modest number of English honours students. And I do not single this out as a whipping boy: there were certainly less worthy treatments of the subject. But looking back, it is of some interest to see what

[1] S. B. Greenfield, *A Critical History of Old English Literature* (London 1966).

Miss Wardale was stressing to those from whom medievalist teachers were recruited.

In discussing the Old English fragments of a poem about Walter of Aquitaine, we might have expected to find Miss Wardale stressing the importance that lies in the conflict of Hagena's loyalties or in the lonely struggle of Waldere and Hildegyth. But what we remember most in her account is the theory that behind not the Anglo-Saxon but the archetypal Walter-story, before it was spread and transmitted in several literatures, lay a sun-myth which leaves its trace in Hildegyth's wakening of her lover each morning to resume the combat—just as (she says) a sun-myth underlies the Old Norse tale of Hildr and Högni, with Hildr able to revivify the slain each morning.

On *Beowulf*, Miss Wardale draws attention to the impressive research in the fifty years from 1880 which saw the assembly of massive information about the poem. 'Gradually', she says, 'one after another of the characters mentioned has been identified with some historical personage. . . . It is even thought that the burial mounds of three of the Swedish kings may be identified near Upsala. . . .' In short, 'the whole composition of the poem has been laid clear'. Thus easily can enthusiasm mislead! No one must of course deny the value of the detailed extraneous information painstakingly amassed. Earlier generations have given us the data which we need for an informed and coherent literary assessment. But Miss Wardale is so carried away by the fifty years' achievement as to think that identifying the 'historical element' (as we came to call it) is of itself to lay clear 'the whole composition of the poem'. And in this, I repeat, she is merely a handy representative of a large-scale critical orthodoxy.

The historical characters are identified. Analogues are found for any fictitious elements that unfortunately and stubbornly remain. The Christian 'element' is isolated from a postulated pagan substratum. The Germanic, Celtic, classical *influences* are itemized with as much objectivity as the times and the PhD supervisor demand. And generations of BA candidates are required to repeat the polaroid task of isolating and itemizing these elements and strata.

Where peripheral discussion of background or textual history gave way to literary assessments of early English literature, these were often painfully naive. Or circular. 'Moralizing', writes one scholar, 'is to be expected in religious poems like the Old English *Elene* or Chaucer's *Prioress's Tale*, but it is found quite as much in such an epic as *Beowulf* and in the romances of a later century'. Here we have a critic first assigning (or at least accepting) genre labels—religious poem, epic, romance—and then plaintively using them as invalidated warranties when poems do not seem to conform to the makers' label. But what are the makers' labels? Half of *Beowulf* was copied by the same monk who preserved *Judith* for us—in which 'moralizing' would presumably be acceptable. What makes the two poems of such different genres that moralizing is not equally acceptable in *Beowulf*? What evidence is there that the Anglo-Saxons regarded *Beowulf* and *Andreas* as of different genres? The latter is also the story of a brave man's adventures, told in closely similar style, informed with similar ideals of heroism and loyalty, and not apparently seeking a very dissimilar response. Although, unlike Beowulf, Andrew is not mourned as dead at the end of the poem, we are asked to share a comparably sickening feeling of loss with those who stood on the sea headland, with grief surging hot in their hearts as they contemplated life without their hero, then departing 'ofer seolhpaðu'. Are there features that are acceptable in *Andreas* which one is to regret as inappropriate in *Beowulf*? By the same token, no system of classifying Anglo-Saxon literature can afford to ignore the fact that, by most of the well-used yardsticks, the Biblical paraphrase *Exodus* is distinctly more heathen, more 'Germanic' and redolent of the migration period, more traditionally 'heroic', its values more in tune with the love of fighting and less with Christian doctrine, than *Beowulf*.

Yet *Beowulf* continued—even continues—to be regarded as inherently early, powerfully reflecting the heroic age, with only a veneer of Christianity in which the name of Christ is studiously avoided. There continued—even continues, despite Tolkien[2] and after—to be overt or covert regret that the poet had squandered his talent on monsters and downgraded to the status of 'digressions' more authentic themes of human love and loyalty (Hildeburh and Finn, Freawaru and Ingeld). We have similarly regretted Cynewulf's *Juliana* in considering the imaginative grace that this poet evinces in *Elene* and *Christ*. So we may feel that the author

[2] J. R. R. Tolkien, 'Beowulf: The Monsters and the Critics', *Proc. Brit. Acad.* 22 (1936).

of *Hali Meiðhad* squandered his talent on a dyspeptic anti-matri-
monial tract when, with realistic vignettes of his neighbours, he
might have anticipated the seventeenth-century imitations of
Theophrastus. Medieval literature has rather consistently suffered
from critics' reluctance to appraise it in terms of the culture that
produced it. And this is as true for the often over-sophisticated
'symbolical' criticism that succeeded Tolkien as for the 'romantic'
criticism that preceded him: the tendency to treat *Beowulf* as a
magnificent hapax, a magnificent failure even, invention in every
line, by a pioneer artist hundreds of years and miles away from a
culture that could have appreciated him: a work as abortive
(though certainly in a different way) as the holograph *Ormulum*
which no-one apparently saw fit to copy and no wonder either.

But this is to ignore the overwhelming evidence of textual
transmission behind Vitellius A 15 which is part of the fifty
years' achievement in *Beowulf* scholarship. The poem is not an
abortive, unappreciated holograph: it had been copied several
times in the generations of its existence before it was bound up
with *Judith* and the *Wonders of the East*. This is the kind of evidence
against which modern critical hypotheses (such as those of Adrien
Bonjour[3] must be tested—or good reason shown why these
patiently-assembled data are no longer valid. In fact, little reason
has been shown why we should belittle the background scholarship as the work of blind mole-like dons grubbing away at
isolated facts, incapable of the grander, synoptic criticism. The
truth is that many of the dons concerned—one thinks for example
of R. W. Chambers—were superlatively capable of the grand
vision and the speculative critical construct; indeed, they had to
school themselves against the temptation to widen their focus
while the need existed for patient and painful assembly of the
often unexciting data which must constitute a prolegomenon
to full critical appraisal. In submitting to which discipline, they
were working in a good tradition: John of Salisbury held that
philology was foster-mother to the study of literature.

Three factors continue to hamper criticism. One is the remoteness of medieval literature from our own time, social context,
and system of values. Secondly, there is the extreme smallness of
the surviving corpus of literature before the fourteenth century.
Thirdly, in part a function of the other two, there is our abiding

[3] *The Digressions in Beowulf* (Oxford 1950).

ignorance of contemporary critical standards and of contemporary consciousness of form and style.

The first of these barriers is the least serious. The cultural remoteness can be countered by exploring the historical background now assembled for this really quite well-documented period. The anonymity of the literary material, of course, is not something that can be circumvented, but the extent to which anonymity contributes to a feeling of remoteness varies very much with individuals. Many feel closer to Chaucer than to the *Gawain*-poet purely because we have biographical information on the one but not on the other. In the case of Anglo-Saxon literature, anonymity is virtually complete. Cynewulf's name is of little help to the literary historian since it is the sole personal detail we have; and of the poet about whom most is known, Cædmon, virtually no work has survived. The anonymity has at least the advantage of sparing us further diversions into peripheral aspects of literature; there are few 'laundry lists' in the period, but how much value in fact are Chaucer's?

The small size of the early corpus is a far more serious handicap, and J. C. van Meurs[4] goes so far as to doubt whether literary judgment is possible at all where the surviving material is so palpably incomplete. But careful estimates of the lost literature have been made, and these cautiously assist us to achieve the perspective we otherwise lack. We know for instance from King Alfred's biographer that it was possible for a child to possess a whole book of English verse in about 850, but no anthology anything like so early has been preserved. We know that not all the work has been preserved even of a poet as highly appreciated in his own time as Chaucer. We have lost his 'Orygenes upon the Maudeleyne' and his book on 'the Wreched Engendrynge of Mankynde, As man may in pope Innocent yfinde', not to mention many balades, roundels, and virelayes. How much more must secular poetry have been neglected at a time when vellum was expensive, the labour of book-making arduous, and when librarians were monks, with predominantly monastic interests? As R. W. Chambers pointed out, 'The Laws of King Edgar forbade a priest to sing [vain songs], even to himself. A competent and energetic librarian, who had found such manuscripts on his shelves, would probably have ejected them as summarily',

[4] *Neophilologus* 39 (1955).

Chambers goes on, with time-bound allusion, 'as a Sunday School superintendent would remove the works of Nat Gould'.[5]

Most serious of all is our ignorance of contemporary taste and canons of literary excellence, though we are by no means entirely in the dark. There is in the first place much material *external* to the early literature that deserves scrutiny for the light it can throw on contemporary standards. The contributions of Bede and Alcuin are rudimentary and largely derivative, but Alcuin's dissertation on rhetoric has considerable interest, as has the treatise on metrics which Bede wrote for a fellow deacon called Cuthbert. Such commentary is of course directed at Latin literature, but references occur to vernacular work and the terms in which the *carmen triviale* is described need to be examined in relation to their use in describing serious Latin verse.

Many early comments are too brief or enigmatic to be of much help. There seems little one can glean from the oft-quoted words of Tacitus when he speaks of *carmina antiqua* in his *Germania*: for one thing they were written almost as many years before the Exeter Book was compiled as have elapsed since this time. And if more interesting, the comments of Sidonius Apollinaris are only doubtfully relevant to English, since his famous scorn is directed at Germanic verse not merely of an earlier era but of a different dialect. 'How can I write this Latin verse', he complains, 'when I live among the long-haired tribes and have to suffer under the weight of Germanic words, and have to praise—however wry-faced—whatever a Burgundian, his hair smeared with stinking fat, chooses to sing?'

But we find hints demanding sensitive interpretation in writers like Ælfric, who wrote fluently in both Latin and English, or Alfred, who wrote both prose and awkward verse in the vernacular, or Aldhelm, whose Latin is now regarded as garrulous and gaudy but whose vernacular poetry (which has not survived) was extravagantly praised in his own time. We have, by the way, an interesting glimpse of an English poet apparently exercising a discriminating taste in replacing some of Aldhelm's grotesque images. The Exeter Book Riddle 40 is a translation of Aldhelm's *De Creatura*, and the Anglo-Saxon poem contains the lines:

> hnescre ic eom   micle halsrefeðre
> seo her on winde   wæweð on lyfte

---

[5] *The Library* 5 (1925).

('softer I am by far than softest down that floats in the breeze') where Aldhelm's Latin had read 'I am softer than cooked tripe'.

Nor should we think of the explicit analyses of metre and rhetoric as being only in Latin. In that remarkable encyclopedic Handbook by Byrhtferð, we find these things set out in English for those with small Latin and less Greek, and there can be no doubt that by the end of the tenth century, at least, native writers consciously applied to the vernacular the stylistic concepts originally expounded only in terms of the classical tongues. Byrhtferð even conceives of barbarisms which sin against the *spoken* vernacular: 'Se ðe his agene spræce awyrt, he wyrcð barbarismum (he who corrupts his own language is committing a barbarism); swylce he cweðe *þu sōt þær* he sceolde cweðan *þu sott.*'

'We wish the student (*se sceawre* 'the seeker') who is studying this treatise', says Byrhtferð, 'to understand with complete clarity that many rhetorical figures (*hiw*) are distinguished in literature (*boccræft*). These are called *figuræ* in Latin and *schemata* in Greek. The first is called *prolepsis* . . . that is in English *fore-stæppung* (stepping in front) or *dyrstynnys* (presumption), when the noun which ought to be behind is in front (þonne se nama byð beforan þe sceolde beon bæftan). The same can be done with verbs.' The extent to which Anglo-Saxon clerkly artists deliberately planned their work with these 'hues' in mind is a promising field of speculation and study.

Even the most oblique comments outside the literature have to be pondered for their bearing on contemporary attitudes and standards. Even the overquoted letter of Alcuin to Hygebald, Bishop of Lindisfarne, is worth fresh contemplation. 'Quid Hinieldus cum Christo' shows not *only* that stories and songs about migration-age heroes were still enjoyed in Christian pre-Conquest England—which we know anyhow from *Beowulf*, *Widsith*, and *Deor*: Alcuin's words have to be read also with the echo they would have for Hygebald who first read them. This rhetorical question is a thematic commonplace from the second century and takes its place with Tertullian's 'What has Athens to do with Jerusalem?' and with Jerome's 'What has Horace to do with the Psalter, or Virgil with the Gospels?' and with that of Honorius of Autun, 'How is the soul profited by the strife of Hector, the arguments of Plato, the poems of Virgil, or the elegies of Ovid?' Ingeld is in good company in this tradition. Alcuin gives us the significant proportional equation, '*As* Aeneas and the heroes of Athens were regarded in the southern Europe of the early Fathers, *so* are Ingeld and the pre-Christian Germanic heroes in eighth-century England.'

And so one could go on multiplying the external sources that can be tapped for information on contemporary standards and attitudes. But we must now turn for a moment to the information that is to be gleaned *internally*, in the literature itself. We are the poorer in having for the native verse form of early England no codified *ars poetica* comparable to that for Latin or Scandinavian verse. Nevertheless the corpus is rich with descriptive and critical terms relating to literature and music which will repay fuller interpretation and evaluation. Consider only the following selection of compounds involving the elements *scop* ('maker, poet'), *leoþ* (cognate with German *Lied*), and *gleo* ('sung music'):

> scopleoð, scopgereord, æfenscop, ealuscop
> leoðcræftig, licleoð, wopleoð (*cf.* geomorgydd), byrgenleoð
>   (*cf.* byrgensong)
> gleobeam, gleowudu, gleomann

Few of these terms are confidently understood: take only *ealuscop*, the 'ale poet', whose work has most regrettably been entirely lost and who is tantalizingly the subject of a legal clause: 'We forbid any priest to be an *ealuscop*.'

Then there are the implications of the many 'experimental' devices we find amid the generally traditional alliterative poetry of Old English. The use of rhyme occurs not only on occasion as the medium for an entire poem, but quite frequently as a sporadic embellishment, as in the *Phœnix*:

> ne forstes fnæst,   ne fyres blæst,
> ne hægles hryre,   ne hrimes dryre

There is fairly extensive play with macaronic verse too:

> se of æþelre wæs   virginis partu
> clæne acenned   Christus in orbem
> metod þurh Marian   mundi redemptor

and in Corpus Christi College, Cambridge, there is a fragment of a poem in this form celebrating Aldhelm, 'beorn boca gleaw, bonus auctor'. More frequently than we commonly suppose, word-play is to be found, as in the Exeter Book Maxims with *treo* 'tree' and *treow* 'faith': 'As trees must surely blossom, so must faith flourish in innocent hearts', a conceit that anticipates by some centuries Marvell's 'vegetable love'.

Lastly, there is formulaic and thematic structure as studied by F. P. Magoun, Jr and others, yielding striking if controversial theories about the composition of early English poetry and valuable implications for contemporary standards of appreciation. It would seem that the audience set great store by the stereotyped image, the traditional epithet, the theme made proper by custom. They appreciated a poet's skill at marshalling the traditional poetic array of phrase and idea. Exiles were always lonely and reflective; meadbenches were places to make resounding vows from; battlefields were the sinister haunt of raven, wolf, and eagle. 'Lo we have heard of the might in days of yore' may today uniquely call *Beowulf* to the minds of the elect among us. Not so in Anglo-Saxon England; in the days of Cynewulf it would have signalled an episodic gambit to be found in any number of poems in the heroic tradition: *Exodus* begins 'Lo we have heard both far and near', *Andreas*, 'Lo we have heard in days gone by'; in both *Elene* and the *Fates of the Apostles*, we find 'Lo we have heard from holy books'; in *Christ*, 'Lo we have heard how Christ himself'; *Juliana* begins, 'Lo we have heard men declare that in the days of Maximian'. No effort at originality obviously: rather, the poet seeks to reassure his audience with the comfortingly familiar. Let one absurd example show how strong was the formulaic urge. In *Andreas* there is a wretched old man who begs to avoid death by offering his son's life; he is a degraded specimen used by the poet to show just how degraded heathendom can be. Yet at this very point he is described as *an old comrade, bold in heart*.

Despite formidable obstacles, then, there is much that can be done by the student approaching the earliest medieval literature today, undeterred by the obsolescent reputation of 'the language side'. We have long since passed from the period when early writings were studied with so great an emphasis upon historical 'philology' and 'background' that 'language' could be equated at one and the same time with medieval history and with 'non-literature'. We have long since entered upon a period in which the language study is no less demanding but in which the goals have become increasingly the critical appraisal of the early writings as literary art.

It remains something of a puzzle that despite the critical insights in the writings of Tolkien and Chambers in the 1930s, of A. G. Brodeur and Dorothy Whitelock in the 1950s, we should in the 1970s find 'language and literature' stubbornly retaining so much of their old double polarity of connotation. Doubtless, it demonstrates the survival of traditional thinking among a sizeable number of those still teaching on 'the language side' of English departments. And it doubtless testifies to the abiding memory of *Beowulf* as a repository of Anglian forms among those who went out to teach English in our schools and warn off the young against the non-literary irrelevance that awaited them at university if they strayed too far on 'the language side'.

5

The Study of the Mother-Tongue

I

It is common practice in inaugural lectures to make to one's predecessors in the Chair some due and proper reference: gracefully, interestingly, piously—and often, indeed, sincerely. It has been my fortune, however, to be honoured with election to two Chairs of which I was to be the first incumbent, and so I have been denied the use of this convenient and appropriate theme. There is, nevertheless, some comfort in even this degree of common ground between the present occasion[1] and my inauguration in Durham. It is not always so, and an earlier Professor of English in this College had a radically different experience. A few years after delivering his inaugural lecture on English studies here, R. G. Latham was reading his inaugural lecture on medicine at the Middlesex Hospital, and the two lectures are printed as the first items in his *Opuscula*, their juxtaposition silently invoking the reader's astonishment. On Professor Latham I wish to say more presently, but the mention of his name at this point fittingly reminds us that, so far from my new Chair representing the beginning of a new study here, teaching and research in the English language have had a long and spectacular history from the early days of the College's foundation to the present time and the distinguished work of Professor A. H. Smith.

The situation which has called this new chair into existence is the awareness—newly acute, but which has been increasing with redoubled momentum since the war—of the central importance of English language studies, not merely in this College and University, not merely in this country, but in the world. We have become better informed about the function of language in society. We have become more concerned about the place of language in

---

[1] This lecture was delivered at University College London on 21 February 1961.

education and about the need for a linguistic discipline, since it is through language that man looks at his world and in fact by means of language that he segments his world. The decline of Latin in our education system has not therefore reduced the need for a linguistic discipline: it has merely added to the responsibilities of the English teacher, as the linguistic discipline comes more and more to have English both as its vehicle and as its object. Moreover, the vastly expanded educational programme of our time means that we must train a far higher proportion of our population than hitherto to make sophisticated use of English in their communication with each other in the higher levels of study, in the arts and sciences alike.

Similarly, the emergence of the underdeveloped countries, both within and without the Commonwealth, has meant not a decrease in the use and teaching of English, but a phenomenal increase, as these countries seek to maintain or establish contact with more advanced areas through the use of the world's chief international language. The situation which C. K. Ogden clearly foresaw between the wars, and for which he ingeniously sought to provide with his British, American Scientific, International, and Commercial form of English, has now fully developed. It was with the manifold problems of this situation in view that the Communication Research Centre was formed here in 1953, and its attention has been focussed on them.

In December 1960, at a Conference of Professors of English, Education, and Linguistics, it was clearly recognized that all the problems just mentioned—even the most formidable and seemingly most remote—are in the last analysis intimately linked with the urgent need to augment and improve the teaching of English, language at all levels in Great Britain. For we must realize that, whether we like it or not, we in this country have special and inescapable responsibilities for the maintenance and propagation of English, responsibilities which devolve upon us by virtue of our history, the Commonwealth, our partnership in the English-speaking world, and—not least—our prestige as the cradle of English. The title of Professor MacKenzie's recent inaugural lecture, *The Outlook for English in Central Africa*,[2] is symptomatic of present concerns and implies a challenge which we must not fail to accept.

[2] Oxford University Press 1960.

II

The position of English today may perhaps assume greater clarity if it is seen in perspective, against the background of Shakespeare's time and the new assertion of the English language. In Richard Mulcaster's England, English was still in competition with Latin on account of the wealth of learning registered in it and because of its value for conferring with other nations. 'Which two considerations being fullie answered', says Mulcaster in 1582,[3] namely 'that we seke [the learned tongues] from *profit* & kepe them for that conference, whatsoeuer else maie be don in our tung, either to serue priuat vses, or the beawtifying of our speche, I do not se, but it maie well be admitted, euen tho in the end it displaced the *Latin*'. As well as having this to say on his age's version of the 'compulsory Latin' question, he interestingly draws attention to the possibility that English may enlarge its scope:

> Will all kindes of trade, and all sorts of traffik, make a tung of account? If the spreading sea, and the spacious land could vse anie speche, theie would both shew you, where, and in how manie strange places, theie haue sene our peple, and also giue you to wit, that theie deall in as much, and as great varietie of matters, as anie other peple do, whether at home or abrode. . . . Now all this varietie of matter, and diuersitie of trade, make both matter for speche, & mean to enlarge it.

Moreover, even if one kept strictly to the facts of the present, even though 'our English tung', as he says, 'is of small reatch, it stretcheth no further then this Ilād of ours, naie not there ouer all'; even though 'our state is no *Empire* to hope to enlarge it by commāding ouer cuntries'; even though the language enshrines 'no rare cunning . . . to cause forenners studie it': nevertheless, it is worth fostering because it is our native tongue.

Within the century that followed, the situation changed radically. English did not remain 'of small reatch', trade and exploration enlarged it in all senses, and there came to be no dearth of foreigners eager to study it. One hundred and fifty years after Mulcaster's death, we find Thomas Sheridan, the dramatist's father, fully alive to what is essentially the modern position and

---

[3] *The First Part of the Elementarie*; quotations are from Ch. 13 and the Peroration.

urging that major steps be taken to meet it. His words have an even greater irony for us than Mulcaster's, for we have been slow to take up his suggestions. In his *Lectures on Elocution*, published in 1762, he sees as a prerequisite for 'the improvement of education' and in consequence 'the benefit of these realms', a thorough 'grammatical knowledge of our mother tongue, and a critical skill therein'. These desired ends will be best achieved, he says, by 'the establishment of these studies at the two Universities; as in those will be found collected all such as are hereafter to be masters of schools, who by learning the English grammar themselves . . . will of course be enabled to teach' it 'throughout the kingdom' (pp. 195–7). Along with these lectures, Sheridan published in 1762 a *Dissertation On the Causes of the Difficulties which occur in learning the English Tongue*, so concerned is he for the foreigners who are seeking to learn English and by the almost total lack of facilities offered them in this country. In the Dedication of this *Dissertation*, he makes a powerful appeal for help to establish an institution 'for the study of the English language'.

To these quotations from Mulcaster and Sheridan, I should like to add one more to complete these notes on the emergence of our present-day situation. It is from the Minute which Macaulay wrote on 2 February 1835, when a decision had to be taken on whether to pursue education in the Indian Sub-Continent through the medium of one of the major oriental languages or whether to turn to English for this purpose:

> We have to educate a people who cannot at present be educated by means of their mother-tongue. We must teach them some foreign language. The claims of our own language it is hardly necessary to recapitulate. It stands pre-eminent even among the languages of the West. It abounds with works of imagination not inferior to the noblest which Greece has bequeathed to us; with models of every species of eloquence; with historical compositions . . .; with just and lively representations of human life and human nature; with the most profound speculations on metaphysics, morals, government, juris-prudence, and trade; with full and correct information respecting every experimental science. . . . Whoever knows that language has ready access to all the vast intellectual wealth which all the wisest nations of the earth have created and hoarded in the course of ninety generations . . . [English] is likely to become the language of com-merce throughout the seas of the East. It is the language of two great

European communities which are rising, the one in the south of Africa, the other in Australasia . . . Whether we look at the intrinsic value of our literature or at the particular situation of [India], we shall see the strongest reason to think that, of all foreign tongues, the English tongue is that which would be the most useful to our native subjects.[4]

As Macaulay's nephew, Sir George Trevelyan, has said,[5] this Minute 'set the question at rest at once and for all', and just as history has endorsed the necessarily limited vision of Mulcaster, so it has the understandably wider one of Macaulay.

III

When Macaulay wrote his Minute, there had been a Chair of English for some years in an English university which was not itself in existence when Sheridan pleaded for the establishment of such studies in Oxford and Cambridge. And four years after Macaulay's Minute, this Chair came to be occupied by that too little remembered scholar, Robert Gordon Latham.

I do not mean that Latham has been forgotten within University College. Professor Smith paid tribute to him in his inaugural lecture eleven years ago, and at the time of the College's centenary his memory was kept alive by Sir Israel Gollancz, Professor R. W. Chambers, and Professor Hale Bellot. But little attempt has been made to assess his place more widely in the history of philology and English language studies. While Holger Pedersen[6] refers very briefly to his attack on the theory of the Asian origin of Indo-European, most historians of our subject make no mention of him at all. It need cause little surprise, therefore, that he is completely ignored in one of the largest and most recent treatments, that of Hans Arens, whose voluminous *Sprachwissenschaft* of 1955 gives due credit to J. V. Stalin and some four hundred others for their services to language study, but who in fact pays scant attention to any British linguist later than Horne Tooke. Yet, for a quarter of a century after his appointment here, Latham was in the very forefront of British linguistics, with a considerable international reputation. He was, as Theodore Watts said, 'one of the first men

---

[4] G. M. Young, *Macaulay: Prose and Poetry* (London 1952), pp. 722–3.
[5] *The Life and Letters of Lord Macaulay* (London 1908), p. 292.
[6] *Sprogvidenskaben i det nittende Aarhundrede* (Copenhagen 1924), p. 293.

inquired after by the celebrity-hunting foreigner in London'.[7] I have thought it fitting, therefore, to single out this one man from among earlier Professors of English here, as deserving our better remembrance in the years ahead.

Latham was born in Lincolnshire, where his father was the Vicar of Billingborough. Like Richard Mulcaster, his great predecessor in the study of English, he went to Eton (of which he became captain) and King's College, Cambridge. Indeed, he is reported as saying that his father marked him from birth for a Fellowship at King's; this parental ambition was realized in 1832, when he was just twenty, and he held it until 1848. Amidst his other early literary activities, he displays his concern for English in a publication which appeared in 1834, entitled *An Address to the Authors of England and America on the Necessity and Practicability of Permanently Remodelling their Alphabet and Orthography*. It begins[8] with somewhat unendearing words which remind us of how uncompromising a man may be at twenty-two: 'The obscurest individual among you . . . works . . . towards the production of what may be called the literature of the age we live in.' Perhaps because so few of his readers were prepared to identify themselves with this 'obscurest individual', Latham's spelling-reform tract appears to have made little impact.[9] Soon after its appearance, he went abroad and studied philology in Germany and Scandinavia, and in Norway he made the acquaintance of a young Manxman, Edward Forbes, three years his junior and the future Professor of Botany at King's College, London. It was perhaps his travels at this time which gave Latham the pseudonym 'Travelling Bachelor' in the 1840s, when he was prominent in a gay circle which included Edward Forbes and Latham's brother-in-law, Edward Creasy, then Professor of History at University College and later knighted. The circle was the Tipperary Hall set, who used to carouse at the Wellington in Highgate, and whose jocular ballads and conversational links were published in *Bentley's Miscellany*. But that is another story.

In 1839 Latham accepted the appointment here as Professor of English, and although he did not retain the Chair for many years, his tenure was of the utmost importance for English and linguistic

---

[7] *Athenæum* (17 March 1888).
[8] According to the abridged copy in the British Museum.
[9] But his *Defence of Phonetic Spelling* of 1872 showed that this was a subject that continued to interest him.

studies both within the College and (especially by reason of the Philological Society) more widely in the country as a whole. Moreover, it was his teaching experience here that fitted him to make the enormous contribution in grammar-writing through which his name became a household word for much of Queen Victoria's reign. While still at University College he pursued medicine along with his other studies and duties, and in 1842 he became a Licentiate (and in 1846 a Fellow) of the Royal College of Physicians. He proceeded to the degree of MD in 1844 and in the same year was appointed Assistant Physician at the Middlesex Hospital, having already been serving there as lecturer in forensic medicine and materia medica. He resigned his Chair here a year later. In 1849 he left the Middlesex Hospital to develop his interest in ethnology, yet a further sphere in which he was to make a notable contribution, and in 1852 he took up duties for a time as Director of the Ethnological Department at the Crystal Palace.

To outline thus sketchily Latham's biography only up to the age of forty, by which time he had achieved both learning and high office in three quite distinct areas of professional life, is enough to show the extraordinary stature of the man: enough to make it seem perfectly natural that by this time, too, he had for some years enjoyed the honour of being a Fellow of the Royal Society. One further scrap of information may help to sharpen the image of his distinction. To show how fortunate Watts-Dunton had been in the company he kept, eight names only are given in the list of great friendships which he enjoyed; the eight are Swinburne, the Rossettis, William Morris, Matthew Arnold, Tennyson, Borrow, Lowell, and Latham.[10]

IV

But of course it is not his life but his contributions to scholarship that I wish to discuss. To be more precise, since he was active and prolific in several fields, I shall restrict discussion to a small selection of his writings. He has to his credit about thirty books alone, and even this is to exclude texts that he merely edited. In addition, between 1844 and 1860 he published more than two dozen papers in the *Reports* of the British Association for the

[10] T. Watts-Dunton, *Old Familiar Faces* (London 1916); all of the circle have attracted biographers, except Latham.

Advancement of Science, of which he remained a member till 1874. During roughly the same period—from 1842 to 1858—he delivered a further and more distinguished two dozen papers to the Philological Society, in the history of which he figured far more prominently than is now generally realized. This was, until Latham's time at University College, a student association, albeit with a rather middle-aged name, The Society for Philological Inquiries. Latham was one of the small band of enthusiasts who contrived to make it the nationwide learned body that it remains today. The change that befell this undergraduate society R. W. Chambers refers to (in an expression which had topical overtones in the twenties) as the 'dictatorship of the professoriate';[11] today we might prefer to call it a 'take-over bid by the directors of the Professorial Board'. Latham was a foundation member of the reconstituted society and a member of the Council for its first eighteen years.

A good many of his articles are on ethnological subjects, and these we must obviously pass over on the present occasion, though it should be remembered that he was, as a contemporary put it, the father of a brilliant school of ethnology, and that he published half a dozen important books in this field, culminating in the two-volumed work, *Descriptive Ethnology*, in 1859. For the rest, his contributions for the British Association and the Philological Society are in various areas of philology: classical philology and prosody; comparative philology; and 'developmental' and 'general' philology—or, as we would usually call them today, historical and general linguistics. On the latter, I should like to draw attention, in passing, to his wealth of writings not only on relatively accessible languages such as those in the Celtic, Slavonic, Ottoman, or even Caucasian groups, but also on American Indian, African, Papuan, and other exotic languages, which established in the Philological Society a tradition of studying the living non-Indo-European languages which has so flourished in our own time, especially with the work of scholars in the School of Oriental and African Studies.

The results of Latham's phenomenally extensive learning in all these fields of philology were brought together in his 700-page volume, *Elements of Comparative Philology*, which was published in 1862 and dedicated to Prince Louis Bonaparte, nephew of

[11] *Philologists at University College* (London 1927), p. 20.

Napoleon the Great and a resident in this country where he was active in linguistic research, particularly in the field of Basque studies. (Through the two millennia from Mithridates to Prince Trubetzkoy, linguistics has been, if not the sport of kings, at least a not infrequent and perfectly respectable hobby of royalty.) It was through this book that he gave widest currency to his theory that the Indo-European languages had their ancient home in Europe rather than in Asia, setting at naught the views of Bopp, Grimm, and Müller, and indeed accusing his opponents (who comprised virtually the entire philological 'establishment') of baseless assumption. His arguments were greeted with scornful incredulity, and there can be no question that his influence and prestige in the most learned circles declined sharply from that time. Theodore Watts, writing Latham's obituary in 1888,[12] says on this point that if it should be found that Latham was right and his opponents wrong, history would find it difficult to assign him too high a place in the scholarly hierarchy of the nineteenth century. Today, most scholars would agree that Latham's opponents were indeed wrong, though history has done little about it and Latham seldom emerges from oblivion except in occasional inaugural addresses.

v

I may well, by this time, have given the impression to those unacquainted with Latham's work that he devoted his energies to almost any study in preference to English, the subject in which he held his Chair at University College. If so, I must hasten to make amends. Latham was deeply interested in both our language and our literature throughout his life, and one might just mention that it is among his very last works that we find the *Two Dissertations on Hamlet*. In his inaugural lecture, delivered on 14 October 1839, he dutifully divided his attention and time between the linguistic and literary programmes on which he discoursed. What he had to say about the study of language on that occasion is not only of the utmost importance for an assessment of Latham: it is also highly relevant to our own times and for the further development of our work.

[12] *Athenæum* (17 March 1888).

In the first place, we must note his insistence that it is contemporary languages that we must study in order to observe philological processes. Such an approach cannot fail, I think, to remind us of that greater linguist, Henry Sweet, who was born in the year of Latham's resignation from the Chair here and whose magnificent contribution to linguistics has been fully and fittingly extolled by C. L. Wrenn[13] and J. R. Firth. Let me read you some words uttered by Sweet in 1877, which Firth loved (as he himself put it) 'to quote in every suitable context'[14]:

> Our tendency is not so much towards the antiquarian philology and text-criticism in which German scholars have done so much, as towards the observation of the phenomena of living languages. . . . Our aim ought clearly to be, while assimilating the methods and results of German work, to concentrate our energies mainly on what may be called 'living philology'.

Beside Sweet's important and forward-looking words, whose place in linguistic history has long been assured, I should like to set these of Latham, spoken in University College nearly forty years earlier:

> We draw too much upon the Philologists of Germany. . . . I believe that the foundations of etymology are to be laid upon the study of existing processes; and I grow sanguine when I remember that by no one as well as by an Englishman can these processes be collected. . . . The details of Etymology I can willingly give up to the scholars of the Continent . . .: but for the *Principles* of Etymology, I own to the hope that it may be the English School that shall be the first to be referred to and the last to be distrusted.[15]

(By 'etymology', one should add, Latham means what we broadly call 'grammar' and he sometimes calls it 'grammatical etymology'; for what we call 'etymology' today, dealing with the individual histories of words, he uses the term 'historical etymology'.) It is noteworthy that the features which make Sweet's words outstanding are here strikingly anticipated by Latham: that, in the era when most energies were devoted to the historical field and when the most exciting philological advances were being made therein,

[13] *Transactions of the Philological Society* (1946), pp. 177–201.
[14] *Trans. Phil. Soc.* (1951), p. 72; see also *Trans. Phil. Soc.* (1946), p. 131, and *Archivum Linguisticum*, 1 (1949), p. 109. Sweet's words are quoted from *Trans. Phil. Soc.* (1877–9), p. 13.
[15] *An Inaugural Lecture* (London 1840), pp. 9, 16–18.

the need should be so clearly felt to strike out in the direction of 'living philology', the observation of 'existing processes'; that an English School should have the temerity to challenge German scholarship; and that this School should specifically seek the principles and systems underlying the mass of details.

There is one further argument which Latham advanced in his inaugural lecture which is also of particular relevance for us today. He claims the 'Sufficiency of the English Language as a Disciplinal Study ... irrespective of the fact of its being the native language of Englishmen'. If we detect here a defensive note arising from the theory of the claim, it has completely gone when Latham returns to this point a year or so later. In *The English Language*, published in 1841, it is not merely that the native language is a *sufficient* study; it is now claimed to be the best. In the first place, he insists that the study of the mother-tongue (and my title today is an echo of his theme) is basic in education: 'With the results of modern criticism, as applied to his native tongue, it is conceived that an educated Englishman should be familiar' (p. v). Secondly, his views have become firmer as to why linguistic studies are best accomplished through the native tongue: 'If it be true that the Theory of a Language is best understood after the Practice of it has been acquired, the fittest disciplinal study in general Grammar, for the native of any country whatever, is the structure of his own Mother-tongue' (p. vii). Again, the Preface to his *English Grammar* of 1843: 'Whatever be the country of the student, the analysis of his native tongue is his best practice in general grammar' (p. vi).

A few years later, in a lecture to the Royal Institution in 1854, he broadens his argument, further endorsing Sheridan's plea which I quoted earlier, and providing us with further reason to renew acquaintance with Latham as these matters assume a new topicality in the context of such present-day talking points as English Language at 'A' Level, and the extension of linguistics in the universities. The lecture was entitled, 'On the Importance of the Study of Language as a Branch of Education for All Classes', and Latham told his audience that 'the study of Speech would find place in a well-devised system of education, even if the tongues of the whole wide world were reduced to a single language, and that language to a single dialect'. Such a view has found increasing favour in recent years: that language study is not merely of relevance in learning a foreign language or the history of one's own language, but in studying any aspect of human behaviour, since language is the most important single characteristic of human behaviour. In the words of Professor James Sledd, which I have quoted on other occasions: 'Man is the speaking animal. That is the main reason for studying speech.'[16] To Latham, too, the value of grammar lies in the scientific study of an instrument, a communication medium; therefore, he says, 'the language which the grammar so studied should represent, must be the mother-tongue of the student. . . . This study is the study of a theory', and since a linguistic theory will be most conveniently pursued if preliminary drills can be dispensed with, it follows that 'a man's mother-tongue is the best medium for the elements of scientific philology'. There is much truth in this, and although it would seem that frequent reference to one's knowledge of at least one foreign language is necessary to gain *the fullest insight* into the structure of one's own, it is surely true nevertheless that the fullest insight into linguistic processes is to be achieved in relation to one's native language, since it is given to few of us to attain comparable *Sprachgefühl* in any other. To this extent Latham is right, and his words emphasize the special responsibility carried by those whose task is to teach the mother-tongue.

VI

We see, then, that even after leaving University College, where he established English language studies on principles which we do well to bear in mind today, he continued to develop his fertile ideas on the place of language studies in education, just as he continued, by his rich contributions, to develop the Philological Society's interests in the directions in which Sweet was later to move with such brilliance and vigour. He came to stress increasingly the geographical spread of English, as for instance in his *Elements of English Grammar for the Use of Ladies' Schools*, which appeared in 1849. Even this little book of a hundred pages, printed in Gower Street, and sold for one shilling and sixpence, begins by describing the world-wide dissemination of English and gives a brief historical account of how this came about. This aspect is further developed in his book, *The English Language*, which in 1862

16 *Language* 34 (1958), p. 139.

appeared in a fifth edition, having grown from a work of just over four hundred pages in 1841 to what is virtually an entirely new book almost twice as extensive. In addition to the relation between British and American English (to this day all too often ignored in our studies), he discusses the English of South Australia —then a recent development—and even such deviant forms of our language as thieves' slang and Taki-taki, a creolized form of English with an admixture of Dutch, spoken in Surinam. The historical statements, moreover, have come to be usefully supported not merely by early forms but by quotations from early grammarians—particularly Wallis, for whom Latham had a high regard. His early insistence on observation of current phenomena has borne fruit in his own increased sophistication in matters such as usage. By 1862, he has grown cool on the value of appeal to the written language, to history, or to scholars; instead he sees usage as determined by imitation, so that one finds one's index rather in 'educated bodies, such as the bar, the pulpit, the senate' because of the 'quantities of imitators that, irrespective of the worth of his pronunciation, each individual can carry with him. On this latter ground', he adds, perhaps with resignation, 'the stage is a sort of standard' (p. 448).

He takes the discussion of usage further in his *Comparative Philology*, again anticipating Sweet in trying to educate public opinion in the direction of an objective approach to language. If language, he says, 'at all times and in all places, stands in the same relation to its ideas as an exponent, it is equally good as language', a view which continues to be misunderstood, though it has been reiterated by Sweet, Bloomfield, and others, from Latham's day to this. While he himself feels that the expression 'bad grammar' is most reasonably to be applied to grammatical statements by a grammarian who has done his work badly, Latham fully sees that such labels are conveniently and inevitably applied with entirely different reference by the speaker of a language from the vantage point of his speech community. But we must understand how parochial, relative, and impermanent that vantage point is. What is called 'bad grammar', says Latham, is a detail in which a speaker differs from someone else who calls *his* form of speech 'good grammar', but imperfect and misguided writings on this subject have confused the issue and obscured the quite separate 'philological truth that *whatever is, is right*'. The man who says *I are*

D

instead of *I am* is reacting to 'unconscious analogies'. While it is true that in England such a speaker would be correctly regarded as belonging to an illiterate stratum of society, yet if such speakers 'formed a community by themselves in (say) an island of the Pacific, and were visited by a missionary there, who formed his grammar solely on what he found . . . the vulgarism would become classical. . . . No one calls *jeg er* bad Danish.' It follows that in itself a development like *I are* 'is as little to be condemned as the conservative force which would have resisted it is to be praised'.[17]

Just as his thinking in general linguistics continued to mature till his later years when we have a small distillation of his accumulated learning in the *Outlines of General or Developmental Philology* (1878), so too on specifically English grammar we find some of his best and most thoughtful work in the slender volume, *Essential Rules and Principles for the Study of English Grammar*, of 1876. It would of course be easy to find fault with his description of English: the grammarian has yet to be born of whom this cannot be said. In all his linguistic work, he tended to be unduly influenced by logic (as witness, in particular, his *Logic and its Application to Language* of 1856), and this frequently mars his handling of English grammar. Moreover, as a product of his age, he is inevitably capable of basing prescriptive statements, particularly in his earlier work, upon largely irrelevant (and sometimes incorrect) historical data. But as early as 1843, he comes near to an 'immediate constituent' analysis of noun phrases like the *king of Saxony's army*, he defines *case* on formal lines which remain acceptable, and for his time makes excellent statements on the function of accent in English.[18] In *A Handbook of the English Language*, which first appeared in 1851, we find such deductions as 'The convertibility of words is in the inverse ratio to the amount of their inflection', and by *inflection* here he means 'peculiar signs expressive of . . . particular parts of speech'; thus a verb *count* can come to be used as a noun more readily than one like *rarify* which has a verb-forming affix. It is of interest to note his disapproval of the terms 'strong' and 'weak', as applied to conjugational distinctions: Sweet so shared his distaste as to replace them by the more descriptive labels 'vocalic' and 'consonantal'. On a point that is more than terminological, Latham observed that 'Notwithstanding its

---

[17] *Elements of Comparative Philology* (London 1862), esp. p. 702.
[18] *An Elementary English Grammar* (London 1843), §§ 296, 307, 312.

name, the present tense, in English, does not express a strictly *present* action',[19] and the modern reader recalls the rediscovery of this fact by descriptive linguists which led some American structuralists to speak of the English tenses as 'past' and 'non-past'.[20]

A later work than the *Handbook* containing interesting observations on English grammar is a fifty-page section of the Preface to the revised edition of *Johnson's Dictionary* which Latham completed in 1866 for Longman, with which firm he had very close relations from about 1860 onwards.[21] He is increasingly concerned to find formal criteria in preference to semantic ones. It is here that we are told that parts of speech can best be distinguished according as words are able to occupy various positions in constructions. It is here, too, that he dwells most thoughtfully on such criteria as accent and frequency of collocation not only to distinguish compound words from word-groups but also to describe the differing degrees of cohesion between words, as in expressions like *make bold*. Again like Sweet after him, he draws attention to an area of linguistic description which falls between the ordinarily conceived provinces of the lexicographer and the grammarian, and he regrets (as we do still) that so little work has been done on it.[22]

VII

The modernity of Latham's thinking, and the recognition that he was tackling educational and linguistic problems which are still with us, naturally lead us to take a brief look at the present. In many ways our situation has grown more complicated: our present educational system and policy make the extension of English-language teaching more urgent than a century ago. In particular, the demand for English teaching overseas has grown immeasurably, and even in those countries with a long and

[19] *A Handbook of the English Language*, 2nd edn (London 1855), §§ 266, 284, 320; this book had run to an eighth edition by 1878.
[20] For example, G. L. Trager and H. L. Smith, Jr, in *An Outline of English Structure* (Norman, Okla. 1951), p. 77.
[21] See Ch. 2 above; the connexion with Longman is also referred to in T. G. Hake, *Memoirs of Eighty Years* (London 1892), where there are interesting notes on Latham, pp. 205 ff.
[22] See my *Essays on the English Language* (London 1968), Ch. 7.

excellent record for teaching English, there is much to be done. The Rev. B. T. Croft has told us of a religious fraternity in Switzerland which appealed for funds from English-speaking travellers by displaying a sign which read: 'The Brothers harbour every kind of disease and have no regard whatever for religion.'[23]

There are of course many good grammars for teaching English to foreigners, but we cannot achieve first-rate ones until we have first-rate grammars for our own use in the English-speaking countries. And these in turn cannot be produced to our proper satisfaction until there has been a major operation in the observation of 'existing processes' in our language, just as Latham recommended in 1839. In the same way, our trustworthy desk-dictionaries today could not have evolved without the immense root-and-branch inquiry into our lexical resources which produced the vast *New English Dictionary*. The Survey of Educated English Usage, which began in Durham and which is now being conducted at University College, seeks to carry out this large-scale observation, and we are fortunate in having the active co-operation of the Talks Division of the BBC (who are understandably concerned to extend knowledge of natural speech behaviour), and of scholars in other universities, both in this country and abroad.

The principles on which the Survey is being conducted are described elsewhere,[24] and it is unnecessary on this occasion to dwell on these. Of the needs which primarily called the Survey into being—the deficiencies at all educational levels in the English-speaking countries—fresh evidence is ever accumulating. On 7 February 1961, *The Times* printed an article on these deficiencies as they related to the United States, deploring the fact that 'More than 94 per cent of the colleges at which elementary school-teachers are training have no systematized study of the history and structure of the English language. More than 61 per cent do not require a course in English grammar and its use.'

Let it not be supposed that we in this country are in an appreciably stronger position, or that educated opinion here is well-informed about the 'existing processes' of English. For the majority of us, what we know about English is what has been handed down by grammatological tradition, and little enough of that was ever based on observation. One small example must

[23] *The English-Speaking World* (September 1960), p. 32.
[24] *Trans. Phil. Soc. 1960*, pp. 40–61.

suffice. Bishop Lowth is typical among the influential early grammarians who insisted that no pause could come between the elements of a simple sentence.[25] Such a pedantic approach to the cadences of spoken English was ridiculed, we remember, by Laurence Sterne:

> —And how did *Garrick* speak the soliloquy last night?—Oh, against all rule, my Lord,—most ungrammatically! betwixt the substantive and the adjective, which should agree together in *number*, *case*, and *gender*, he made a breach thus—stopping, as if the point wanted settling;—and betwixt the nominative case, which your lordship knows should govern the verb, he suspended his voice in the epilogue a dozen times, three seconds and three-fifths by a stop-watch, my Lord, each time. . . .—But in suspending his voice—was the sense suspended likewise? . . . I look'd only at the stop-watch, my Lord.

Small wonder that this and similar instances of uninformed criticism cause Tristram Shandy, Gent., to exclaim: 'Grant me patience, just heaven!—Of all the cants which are canted in this canting world . . . the cant of criticism is the most tormenting!'[26]

One would hesitate to apply such immoderate language to criticism at the present time, but at least one able and generally perceptive critic of the spoken word has recently expressed views on pauses which are not at all dissimilar to those of the critic in *Tristram Shandy*. Attacking the speech-habits of television commentators and interviewers, Mr Hilary Corke particularly objects to 'the breaking up of sentences into wholly unnatural units', as when a writer is introduced 'whose first. Book has been translated into. Fourteen languages and he's. John Braine the author of. *Room at the Top*.'[27] Nor is it only critics who are thus influenced by the logic of arrangements of words as clustered and punctuated in the written forms of English. The Polish linguist Wiktor Jassem, phonetician and author of one of our best analyses of English intonation, uses such terms as 'anomalous pause' and 'misfit of a rhythmical character' of breaks like those that Mr Corke criticizes as 'unnatural'. One of Dr Jassem's examples is 'apart from. snakes'.[28]

[25] *A Short Introduction to English Grammar* (London 1762), p. 161.
[26] *Tristram Shandy* (London 1761), III, Ch. 12.
[27] *The Listener* (26 November 1959).
[28] *Intonation of Conversational English* (Wrocław, 1952), pp. 40, 91, 98.

VIII

Now, it would certainly appear that when someone reads aloud from the printed page, he pauses at the punctuation points rather than at these so-called 'unnatural' places. But, of course, written English read aloud is not the most typical kind of spoken English. In the impromptu speech being examined in the Survey, pauses between subject and verb, verb and object, preposition and noun are—under certain conditions—too common with all types of speakers to be designated 'unnatural' or 'anomalous', and so far as these pauses show a characteristic distribution, this distribution must appear in our description. It may well be that Mr Corke's interviewers, in trying to act a natural conversational style, over-play a single feature which they have noticed. This is a rather common state of affairs when so little objective description exists of our stylistic strata, and one must expect fictional dialogue to be in some respects more 'colloquial' than actual speech, or the village councillor to be more parliamentary than a front-bench MP.

So little, in fact, is generally known about the caesuras of speech, after generations of orientation towards written English, that Mr Allen Ginsberg and other Beat poets are able to form the impression that they are almost alone in observing them. In a discussion with Mr Carne-Ross in the 'Art—Anti-Art' series on the radio a little time ago, Mr Ginsberg made the extraordinary claim that the breaks and halts and so-called 'syntactic dissociations' in the Beatitude poetry represent not merely a change from the poetical tradition but an actually new speech, American speech, first properly heard and exploited in poetry by William Carlos Williams early this century. I need not now stop to illustrate these linguistic features in the work of Ginsberg and his colleagues: indeed, even in these post-Chatterley days, it is not very easy to select continuous passages from such verse that could be passed as suitable for adult audiences. I call Ginsberg's statement extra-ordinary, not because his poetry does not evince these phenomena, but because he thinks they are a recent development, American, and newly exploited in verse.

In his *Lectures on the Art of Reading*, of 1775, Thomas Sheridan —whom I quoted earlier—gave a warning that the enjoyment of verse was marred by an adherence to the sentential punctuation of the written form. If one failed to pause at the end of a run-on line, one failed to mark the correlation effect between the end of that line and the end of its neighbour, a correlation which, he said, was not for the eye only (II, pp. 102 ff.). But this means admitting in some of our best poetry, pauses of the kind that have been called 'unnatural' and 'anomalous', only recently admitted to verse, and even American. In Keats's *Lamia*, for instance,

> For the first time, since first he harboured in
> That purple-lined palace of sweet sin

or Blake's *Evening Star*

> The fleeces of our flocks are covered with
> Thy sacred dew: protect them with thine influence

we have breaks between prepositions and noun phrases, rather as in the criticized examples which I have quoted: 'the author of. *Room at the Top*' and 'apart from. snakes'. This is one of the positions in which a break has been most insistently held to be inadmissible,[29] even by those elocutionists of the late eighteenth century who deplored the restriction of pauses to positions admitting a punctuation mark; Walker states specifically that 'the *preposition* and the *noun* it governs' are 'too intimately connected to admit a pause'.[30] Such a view would naturally be upheld by the traditional equation of the English prepositional phrase with the Latin noun in oblique cases. As we have seen, however, this runs counter to the evidence in our prosody and to the evidence of the distribution of pauses in present-day speech. On the contrary, our observations show that, in the formation not only of clauses but also of phrases, pauses play a role—along with other features like tempo, pitch, and prominence—in indicating relative coherence within groups of words which function as units. This may mean that, as well as appearing at points of lexical selection (as so valuably described by a colleague at University College, Dr Goldman-Eisler,[31] pauses occur in such utterances as 'apart from. snakes' and 'covered with. dew' by virtue of being at the terminals

[29] There are, however, one or two instances acknowledged by the outstanding observer, Joshua Steele, in *An Essay Towards Establishing the Melody and Measure of Speech* (London 1775).
[30] *Elements of Elocution* (London 1781), p. 26.
[31] See, for example, *Language and Speech* 1 (1958), pp. 226–31.

of grammatical selection.[32] In other words, a means is offered of distinguishing between expressions having prepositions as proclitic to a following nominal word and expressions having prepositions as grammatically determined enclitics, these being in the category which has caused the emergence of locutions like 'he used to' and 'a house to dream of', and which interested Latham when he was contemplating the relative cohesion of words in recurrent collocations.

Even if time allowed, this would not be the occasion to venture further into the technicalities of English grammar. I have said enough, I hope, to stress how much must be done to extend our critical awareness of our own language, how urgent is the need to press on with work in this field, and how inspiring are our College traditions in the study of the mother-tongue. But with some misgiving I recall now the American linguist Edward Sapir, who once said that the man who elects to talk about grammar 'is regarded by all plain men as a frigid and dehumanized pedant'. If it is already too late to dissuade my students from agreeing with all plain men on this, I can at least hope that they have not been driven to the lengths of agreeing also with Richard Mulcaster that 'a mere grammarian is but a poor mean to do anie thing well, euen where he professeth most'.

[32] See the useful data in Б. Н. Аксененко, Предлоги Английского Языка (Moscow 1956), and the statement of relationships, p. 5.

6

Dasent, Morris, and Aspects of Translation

Translation is one of the most difficult tasks that a writer can take upon himself, and the problems with which he is confronted far transcend linguistic comprehension.[1] One of the main obstacles that seems to have inhibited the growth of an adequate body of doctrine on the subject, a theory and criticism of translation, is that the difficulties vary profoundly according to the manifold combinations of source- and target-languages involved. In translating contemporary languages, for example, it matters a great deal whether we are concerned with languages remote genetically, spatially, and culturally (as English and a Polynesian or American-Indian language), or languages closely related, whose speakers are neighbours, sharing to some extent a single culture (as for example the languages in Belgium, or Switzerland, or South Africa, or Wales).

At the one extreme, we are dealing with languages whose structures differ so much that to use King Alfred's expression, translation 'word be worde' is quite impossible, and 'andgit of andgite' possible only if we deal in large sense-units. 'In this case,' as Joseph Priestley put it, 'intire words resemble single letters in other words: that is, they have no meaning in themselves, but the phrase composed out of them is the least significant part into which the sentence it helps to form can be divided; as, in general, single words are the least significant parts of a sentence.'[2] Here is a problem extensively handled in the writings of Benjamin Lee Whorf and others. And often, on top of this, we lack the cultural

---

[1] Reprinted, with some revision, from *Saga-Book* 14 (1955).

[2] *A Course of Lectures on the Theory of Language and Universal Grammar* (Warrington 1762), p. 231; Priestley discusses several important aspects of translation in this book, especially on pp. 227–34.

correlates to make translation possible, and we resort to the more or less arbitrary use of technical terms, defined in footnotes which must needs describe the unfamiliar institution in question. Even at the other extreme—English and Welsh, or Flemish and French—we are deceived if we imagine that we are concerned merely with a single set of referents for which there are exactly equivalent labels available in the two languages; the cultural difficulty may trouble us less, but it is still there, since it is probable that there is never an absolute identity of culture where there is not identity of language.[3] The French and the English peoples have been close neighbours (and sometimes rather more) for a millennium and a half, yet we had no word that could translate General de Gaulle's '*Rassemblement* du Peuple Français'.

Translating the languages of past ages presents the same problems but in a considerably aggravated form, since in estimating all meanings we are restricted to sitting mutely before a relatively small—and ineluctably finite—body of writings, instead of enjoying a two-way traffic with the expansiveness of readily available data that we have in a contemporary, living language. This erects what is at times an unassailable barrier to gauging the niceness of flavour imparted by a word's rarity or familiarity, its literary, venerable, or colloquial associations, and to determining the nature and significance of unfamiliar habits and institutions. Indeed, even when we have gained an adequate working knowledge of both language and culture of ancient Greece or saga-age Iceland or medieval England, we are left with the incommunicability of the culture as an unsolved problem. With stubborn exceptions like *thou* and *ye*, Chaucer's grammatical forms can usually be replaced by forms which will be understood by present-day English speakers, but what are we to do with such things as pardoners and summoners and reeves? Even clerks are not what they were. And if we latinize or euphemize four-letter words which once amused rather than shocked, are we translating accurately?

But this phrase 'translating accurately' brings us to the heart of the problem. What, after all, is accuracy in translation?

Both Dasent and Morris reckoned themselves to be accurate

---

[3] Cf. E. Sapir, 'Language and Environment', *American Anthropologist* 14 (1912), pp. 226–42, and references in E. H. Lenneberg, 'Cognition in Ethnolinguistics', *Language* 29 (1953), pp. 463 ff.

translators: they were so reckoned by their contemporaries, and no-one would want to change that verdict today. Yet the difference between the work of these two scholar-translators is profound, and it reveals a difference of approach to the art of translating which is just as profound and which is the subject of the present paper. Let us remind ourselves of the contrasting styles of Dasent and Morris by considering a brief excerpt not from the early but from the mature work of each. First, from the famous translation of *Njála*, on which Dasent tells us he worked on and off for eighteen years:

'Shew me to Njal's sons', said the Earl, 'and I will force them to tell me the truth.'

Then he was told that they had put out of the harbour.

'Then there is no help for it', says the Earl, 'but still there were two water-casks alongside of Thrain's ship, and in them a man may well have been hid, and if Thrain has hidden him, there he must be; and now we will go a second time to see Thrain.'

Thrain sees that the Earl means to put off again and said,—

'However wroth the Earl was last time, now he will be half as wroth again, and now the life of every man on board the ship lies at stake.'

They all gave their words to hide the matter, for they were all sore afraid. Then they took some sacks out of the lading, and put Hrapp down into the hold in their stead, and other sacks that were light were laid over him.

Now comes the Earl, just as they were done stowing Hrapp away. Thrain greeted the Earl well. The Earl was rather slow to return it, and they saw that the Earl was very wroth.[4]

---

[4] G. W. Dasent, *The Story of Burnt Njal* (Edinburgh 1861) II, 30. The corresponding Icelandic is as follows:

Jarl mælti: 'Vísi mér til Njálssona—ok skal ek nauðga þeim til, at þeir segi mér hit sanna.' Þá var honum sagt, at þeir höfðu út látit. 'Ekki má þat þá', segir jarl, 'enn vatnkeröld tvau váru þar við skipit Þráins, ok má þar maðr vel hafa fólgizt í. Ok ef Þráinn hefir fólgit hann, þá mun hann þar í hafa verit. Ok munu vér nú fara í annat sinn at finna Þráin.' Þráinn sér þetta, at jarl ætlar enn út, ok mælti: 'Svá reiðr sem jarl var næstum, þá mun hann nú vera hálfu reiðari—ok liggr nú við líf allra manna þeira er á skipinu eru.' Þeir hétu allir at leyna; því at hverr varum sik mjök hræddr. Þeir tóku sekka nakkvara ór búlkanum, enn létu Hrapp koma þar í staðinn—fóru nú aðrir sekkar á hann ofan, þeir er lettir váru. Nú kemr jarl, er þeir höfðu um Hrapp búit. Þráinn kvaddi vel jarl. Jarl tók kveðju hans ok ekki skjótt. Sá þeir at jarl var allmjök reiðr.

(*Njáls Saga*, ed. Vald. Ásmundarson (Reykjavík 1894), pp. 206 f.)

Beside this let us place the following excerpt from Morris's noble version of *Eyrbyggjasaga,* published thirty years later than *Burnt Njal* but showing no essential features different from the *Grettis Saga* which belongs to the same decade as the work of Dasent already quoted:

'That may be', said Arnkel, 'but we will have a ransacking here.'

'That shall be as ye will', said Katla, and bade her cook-maid bear light before them and unlock the meat bower, 'that is the only locked chamber in the stead.'

Now they saw, how Katla span yarn from her rock, and they searched through the house and found not Odd; and thereafter they fared away.

But when they were come a short space from the garth, Arnkel stood still and said:

'Whether now has Katla cast a hood over our heads, and was Odd her son there whereas we saw but a rock?'

'She is not unlike to have so done', said Thorarin, 'so let us fare back.' And that they did.

But when it was seen from Holt that they turned back, then said Katla to her women:

'Ye shall still sit in your seats, but I will go with Odd out into the fore-chamber.' So when they were come through the chamber door, she went into the porch against the outer door, and combed Odd her son, and sheared his hair.[5]

I should like to draw attention to some points in these excerpts which are characteristic of the two great translators we are considering and which may clarify what I have to say later. In the first passage, the adjective *wroth* strikes us today as perhaps old-

---

[5] W. Morris, E. Magnússon, *The Story of the Ere-Dwellers* (London 1892) 45 f.   The corresponding Icelandic is as follows:

'Vera má þat', segir Arnkell, 'enn rannsaka viljum vér hér.' 'Þat skal sem ýðr líkar', segir Katla, ok bað matselju bera ljós fyrir þeim ok lúka upp búri; þat eitt er hús læst á bænum. Þeir sá, at Katla spann garn af rokki. Nú leita þeir um húsin ok finna eigi Odd, ok fóru brott eftir þat. Ok er þeir kómu skamt frá garðinum, nam Arnkell staðar ok mælti: 'Hvárt mun Katla eigi hafa heðni veift um höfuð oss? ok hefir þar verit Oddr son hennar er oss sýndist rokkrinn.' 'Eigi er hon ólíkleg til', segir Þórarin, 'ok förum aftr.' Þeir gerðu svá. Ok er sást ór Holti, at þeir hurfu aftr, þá mælti Katla við konur: 'Enn skulu þér sitja í rúmum yðrum, enn vit Oddr munum fram ganga.' Enn er þau koma fram um dyrr, gekk hon í öndina gegnt útidyrum ok kembir þar Oddi syni sínum, ok skerr hár hans.

(*Eyrbyggja Saga*, ed. Vald. Asmundarson (Reykjavík 1895), pp. 40 f.)

fashioned, but in Dasent's time it was not so tinged with archaism and was commonly encountered in popular novels; in his time, too, the past participle *hid* was still very common beside the analogical formation *hidden*,[6] and so would not be obtrusive to his readers. On the other hand, the use of *sore* in the expression *sore afraid* was already thoroughly archaic in the mid-nineteenth century. One should take note, perhaps, of the good nautical terms *lading* for 'cargo' and the verb *stow away* for placing goods in position aboard ship; and one might notice too the use of such idioms as 'there is no help for it' and 'to give one's word', simply because of their thoroughly familiar character. The most striking feature of Dasent's style, indeed, is that there is little that is striking in it; above all, we note that no syntactical expression here differs from the normal English of educated nineteenth-century usage.

Morris's language on the other hand contains much that is remarkable to us and much that must have been remarkable to his contemporaries too; for example, the rare technical sense of *ransack*, the rarer of the two preterite forms of *spin*, the obsolete and poetical use of *fare* in the sense of 'go', the archaic *rock* for 'distaff', the fairly rare *garth*. Perhaps more notable than these is *whereas* in the sense of 'where', a favourite form with Morris but with few other writers in recent centuries; and we should add here the use of *bower* which is clearly a translation-loan, and the expression *not unlike to* which is similarly a close imitation of the Icelandic. Above all, we have *whether* introducing a direct question; this idiom, which fell into disuse in the sixteenth century, was never a common feature of English, but was in any case characterized by a different word-order from that used by Morris here. Morris's use of *whether* with inversion of subject and verb is again directly modelled on the Icelandic idiom.[7]

Enough has been said to show some of the most obvious areas in which the translation styles of Dasent and Morris differ from each other. It has been common to sum up, even to explain,

[6] Cf. O. Jespersen, *A Modern English Grammar* (London 1954), VI, p. 58.
[7] Other examples could be cited from the excerpt presented, and even more striking ones from elsewhere in *The Story of the Ere-Dwellers*; cf. 'door-doom' (*duradómr*), 'overtrue is that' (*of satt er þat*), 'then shall we take that for sooth' (*þá munum vér þat fyrir satt hafa*), p. 34, 'handsel me now the land' (*handsala mér nú landit*), 'that shall not be before every penny is first yolden' (*eigi skal þat fyrr enn hverr penningr er fyrir goldinn*), p. 24.

these contrastive styles in terms of archaism and romanticism. Exponents of the two main traditions of translation which sprang severally from Dasent and Morris have regarded themselves— and have been regarded by others—as using on the one hand English that is contemporary, natural, and prosaic, or on the other hand English tha tis evocatively archaic, romantic, and poetic.[8] But this is to oversimplify the difference of approach. In any case, it is not strictly accurate to contrast Dasent and Morris as respectively contemporary and archaic in style. Dasent is praised by a reviewer in 1866 for his 'old-world diction' which is one of the factors contributing to make his style for the sagas 'very near perfection';[9] and while most contemporaries notice with approval or disapproval Morris's 'archaism' and 'quaintness'. Sir Edward Gosse is to be found praising him for his 'pure, simple and idiomatic English'.[10]

Certainly, although Dasent speaks of withstanding the temptation to use old words and expressions,[11] he does not in fact eschew them. Forms like 'sore afraid' (which we have noticed above) and 'this was noised about' occur on every page, and they have pleased successive generations of readers, as they pleased his contemporaries, with the air of sobriety and dignity that they impart through their almost Biblical ring. By contrast, many of the most striking and unfamiliar words in Morris are not, properly speaking, archaisms at all: they are rather cases of the re-introduction, with new pronunciations and often with new meanings and into new environments, of words or word-elements from a past so distant that they are virtually new words to the modern reader. One did not call the word *biologie* an archaism when Jean Lamarck coined it in 1815, for all that it was made up of elements of great antiquity, and such native formations as William Barnes's *hearsomeness* for 'obedience', or *forestoneing* for 'fossil', were just as 'new' as the word *telephone* which was coined at about the same time.

Nor were the syntactical constructions or word-order patterns

---

[8] Cf. Richard Beck, *Modern Language Notes* 46 (1931), p. 485, who praises the 'fluent and idiomatic English' of Halldór Hermannson, *Islendingabók*, in contrast to the 'artificial and antiquated language' of Vigfusson and Power, *Origines Islandicae.*

[9] *Spectator* (14 April 1866).

[10] *Academy* (17 July 1875), pp. 54–5.

[11] Cf. footnote to p. xv, *Burnt Njal* I.

in Morris so much archaic as entirely unfamiliar to the nineteenth-century reader. Moreover, they are more directed to simulating the original from which Morris was translating than recapturing arrangements popular in an earlier form of English. The same is true of the so-called archaism in those who have pursued the Morris tradition. The impressively artistic volume prepared by the Chiswick Press which contains Robert Proctor's version of *Laxdælasaga*[12] begins: 'Ketil Flatneb hight a man', using a word-order which had never been common in English even at the time when *hight* was a common enough form. But it is, of course, as close a translation as is conceivable of the Icelandic 'Ketill flatnefr hét maðr'—every word being replaced by a cognate form which is either English now or has been, sometime, somewhere. On the same page, Proctor tells us that Ketill 'summoned a thing' and 'thus hove up his tale'. Similarly, although E. R. Eddison's defence of archaisms is spirited enough to be an apologia,[13] what strikes us most in his able and challenging work is not so much archaisms as neologisms in the shape of unfamiliar foreign idioms dressed in English garb. For example, 'Sought they then to Thorfinn's at eventime, and gat there all good welcome'. And again, 'Parted they with things in such case. Fared Arinbiorn home and said unto Egil his errand's ending. . . . Egil became all frowning: seemed to himself to have lost much fee there, and nowise rightfully.' As Dr Edith Batho says of this translation, Norse English cannot in itself be any more desirable than the Latinate English that Eddison condemns in some of his pre-decessors; it may in fact be less comprehensible, so far as the general reading public is concerned. Because English and Ice-landic are 'akin in word, syntax and idiom', she says, we are in danger of regarding them as identical: 'Fared they back' may be close to normal Icelandic syntax but it is not normal English syntax and can only give an ordinary English reader the improper impression that the sagas are mannered.[14] Dr Batho's reference here to 'Norse English' is thus far more apt than the criticism of another reviewer who spoke of Eddison's using an archaic 'dialect . . . going back even beyond the age of Biblical English'.[15]

[12] *The Story of the Laxdalers* (London 1903).
[13] *Egil's Saga* (Cambridge 1930), pp. 239–41.
[14] *Modern Language Review* 27 (1932), pp. 231 f.
[15] *New Statesman* 36 (1930), p. 364.

The point is that Eddison's 'dialect' does not go back to an English earlier or later than 'the age of Biblical English': whether consciously or not, Eddison was composing in a new English idiom, based closely upon Icelandic.

The mention of the Bible reminds us that the Authorized Version likewise contains much that is neither the English of 1611 nor that of an earlier period, but a synthetic blend of archaism and imitation of foreign idiom, with a fair seasoning of what the translators themselves felt was a form of English appropriate to be the vehicle of the Word of God. Dr E. V. Rieu points out, in an important essay, that the starkness and reality of the Greek are to some extent lost in the Authorized Version, which was reproducing to a marked extent the older English of Coverdale and Tyndale: it was therefore 'already old-fashioned when it was written'. But, he says, it is far from being simply archaic. 'Unlike the Greek, it was not firmly based on the normal speech of its own or any other period'. As an example, Dr Rieu cites St Luke 17.8 where the Greek has a colloquial and not particularly polite demand which may be translated as 'Get something ready for my supper': the Authorized Version reads, 'Make ready wherewith I may sup'. While conceding that the words of the AV here 'follow the Greek with some exactitude', Dr Rieu says 'I contend that no Englishman alive in 1611 or at any other date would have used such an expression.'[16] The beauty of the Authorized Version as against that of other translations is not in question: it is simply a matter of a different approach to translating, and it is to some extent paralleled in the different approaches of Dasent and Morris to translating the sagas.

But so far we have been considering only the different realizations of these contrasting approaches and not the approaches themselves. Earlier, we mentioned that it is commonly held that Morris's position contrasted with Dasent's in being romantic. But although Morris's work bears abundant signs linguistically of that glorification of things medieval and 'Gothick' which characterized the English Romantic movement, romanticism alone is not sufficient to mark him off from Dasent. Like Morris, Dasent too had a passionate regard for the literature, culture, and institutions of the medieval North: indeed, he had an unreasoning love for them which to some extent denied him the

16 *The Four Gospels* (London 1952), pp. x–xi.

facility of objective appraisal. One need mention in this connexion only his free and romantic handling of the *Jómsvíkinga-
saga*[17] which matched other mid-Victorian novels in more ways
than in running to three volumes, and which only a foster
parent's devotion could have induced him to call a 'very amusing
story'. In his address to the reader, he is very far from being the
prosy and uninspired writer that Eddison took him to be,[18]
inviting the reader as he does to escape with him from humdrum
nineteenth-century existence—'for I will not call it life'—and to
come 'far far away' into the Scandinavian North of the tenth
century. A romantic regard for Old Scandinavia will not readily
distinguish Morris from Dasent.

Where they differ in their approach to the sagas is over what a
translation should be. Dasent sought to make his translation only
as literal 'as the idioms of the two languages would permit'. As a
general rule, he says, he 'has withstood the temptation to use Old
English words' and has been determined to avoid expressions
'which are not still in every-day use', though he admits to some
lapses from such rigorous principles, namely, *busk, boun,* and *redes*.[19]
He has learnt a great deal in the eighteen years during which he has
been working on *Burnt Njal*, and in the nineteen years since he read
Carl Säve's lengthy review[20] which took him severely to task for
the artificial and antiquarian diction in his translation of the
Prose or Younger Edda published in Stockholm in 1842:

> Almickle in himself is Utgard's Loki, though he deals much with
> sleight and cunning spells, but it may be seen that he is great in
> himself, in that he has thanes who have mickle might. (p. 66)

He is now of the opinion that 'The duty of a translator is not to
convey the sense of his original in such a way that the idioms and
wording of one tongue are sacrificed to those of the other, but to
find out the words and idioms of his own language which answer
most fully and fairly to those of the language from which he is
translating, and so to make the one as perfect a reflection as is
possible of the forms and thoughts of the other.'

[17] *The Vikings of the Baltic* (London 1875).
[18] *Egil's Saga*, p. 232.
[19] *Burnt Njal* I, pp. xiv–xv.
[20] In *Frey* (Uppsala 1842), pp. 389–97. For this and other references to
review literature, I am indebted to Halldór Hermannsson's invaluable
bibliographies in *Islandica*.

As a statement of principle, it is not of course very helpful to talk of making 'the one as perfect a reflection as is possible of the forms and thoughts of the other', but read in the context of his actual work, Dasent's aim is perfectly clear, despite the fact that it was by no means always realized. Such an aim was expressed more succinctly and scientifically by E. V. Rieu in a lecture on his own principles of translation, read before the London Medieval Society some years ago, when he talked of 'the principle of equivalent effect'. A full definition of Rieu's approach is printed in *Cassell's Encyclopedia of Literature* (London 1953, I, p. 555), where it is stated that 'that translation is the best which comes nearest to creating in its audience the same impression as was made by the original on its contemporaries'. Similarly, Sir H. Idris Bell has said that a translator's aim should be to 'produce on readers in his own tongue an effect corresponding as nearly as maybe with that received by readers of the original'.[21] At the same time, commenting upon Dryden's claim 'to make Virgil speak such English as he would have himself spoken, if he had been born in England and in this present age', he points out that this cannot be pressed too far; Virgil as a seventeenth-century citizen of England is in fact an impossible concept, since his writings will have him no other than a Roman of the Augustan Age.[22]

Dasent sought to make his translation have upon English-speaking readers the same effect as the sagas had, not upon Icelanders of the nineteenth century, but upon Icelanders of the age at which they were written. Some question-begging is of course involved here, but this would be less obvious in Dasent's time than in our own, after a generation of controversy over the dating, historicity, and mode of transmission of the sagas. For Dasent's purposes, he had simply to achieve an effect equivalent to that upon an age when language, morals, and culture had changed little if at all from the age in which the events narrated had taken place.[23] At the same time, he does not attempt to introduce such

---

[21] 'The Problem of Translation' (*Literature and Life*: *Addresses to the English Association*, London 1948), p. 23.

[22] *Ibid.*, pp. 25–6.

[23] If his basic assumption is that an old text was intended to have an archaic flavour and antiquarian interest for contemporary readers, the translator's task is naturally immensely complicated: cf. J. R. R. Tolkien in *Beowulf . . . A Translation . . .* by J. R. Clark Hall (London 1940), pp. xiv–xv.

idiom of fashionable contemporary colloquy as we might today if
we were applying the principle of equivalent effect to a translation of Jean Anouilh: he was a writer too sensitive to lapse into
the incongruities that would be presented if Gunnar, armed with
bow and arrow in the defence of his life, were to talk in idiom
inextricably associated in the nineteenth-century reader's mind
with the Siege of Delhi, factory acts, or steam trains. He therefore
seeks his equivalence of effect in English words and idiom which
are as far as possible timeless and unobtrusive, bearing no outstanding associations with institutions antique or contemporary.[24]
His success is shown in a small way by his consequent ability to
mark off a proverb (having presumably a distinctive, antique
effect on a medieval reader) from the main text by couching it in
quaint and gnomic form utterly different from his style elsewhere:
'Bare is back without brother behind it.'

A language from which we are translating may hold such a
fascination for us that we want to reproduce its every verb,
compound, and syntactical arrangement with an image which is as
faithful as the camera of our own linguistic genius can photo-
graph it: we want our reader to taste the same sequence of exotic
semantic delights in his interpretation of our translation as we
ourselves taste in the original. The word 'exotic' is crucial here.
There is a difference between knowing a language so well that it
is perfectly comprehensible and knowing a language as a native
speaker of it. In the former case we can still feel an exotic experience in the order, for example, in which words impinge on our
consciousness: in the latter, they are blurred into an unanalysable
cliché. 'Ketill flatnefr hét maðr' can be 'Ketil Flatneb hight a
man' to a Proctor, a Morris,[25] or an Eddison,[26] but not to a

---

[24] This is not to say that Dasent's style, for all its fame, was more timeless
and unobtrusive than that of every other nineteenth-century translator. The
history sagas have for the most part been consistently approached with
far less self-consciousness and striving after special effect than the more
popular and 'literary' family sagas; if 'timelessness' is taken as an indication
of equivalence of effect, the laurels should no doubt go to Jón Hjaltalín and
Gilbert Goudie for *The Orkneyinga Saga* (Edinburgh 1873). It is significant
that the aim of this volume was to present an annotated historical source-
book and not a piece of literature.

[25] 'Ketil Flatneb was hight a famous hersir' (*Ketill flatnefr hét einn ágætr
hersir*), *The Story of the Ere-Dwellers*, p. 3.

[26] 'S. and H. hight two brethren' (*S. ok H. hétu brœðr tveir*), *Egil's Saga* 32;
cf. 'Biorgolf was named a man' (*Björgólfr hét maðr*), *ibid.* 9.

Halldór Hermannsson,[27] and we find Stéfan Einarsson saying of Eddison's *Egil's Saga*, 'to me the language of the translation looked a bit more old-fashioned as English than the language of the original is as Icelandic.'[28] It is as though a translation of the Canterbury Tales were to seem to us less familiar and idiomatic than Chaucer's own words.

This then is where Morris's approach, as I see it, differs from Dasent's. So far from trying to make his translation convey to his readers an equivalent effect to that conveyed by the sagas to medieval Icelanders, he seeks a transmission of his own experience. He wants to make us share the acute pleasure which the forms and arrangements of the Icelandic have upon him. His readers must be made to share the magic experience of a remote literature, dealing with a remote culture in a remote language. They must read the sagas with just that extra concentration and care that Morris himself had to use. They must find them couched in a language which would be as intelligible to them as Icelandic was to him but which would have the same areas of unfamiliarity too. As one nineteenth-century critic put it admiringly if unflatteringly, Morris's 'quaint' English 'has just the right outlandish flavour'.[29] To Morris, as to Eddison, it was a translators' task to tell his readers 'something about' the original, to show them not 'his judgement' but 'his original'.[30]

For this reason, it is not strictly to the point to say, as some twentieth-century critics have said, that Morris's translations are difficult to read *nowadays* 'because of the obsolescent language'.[31] Morris's work can scarcely be more difficult to read now than it was in the nineteenth century nor his language be more obsolescent. Since his forms are not tied as consciously to the nineteenth century as even Dasent's were, it could even be argued that his translations have dated less. At any rate, 'easy reading' was less Morris's aim than the poetic transmission of his own experience.

We would not wish to grade these two great translators, and we could not if we wished. Their public and their disciples and their disciples' public have amply demonstrated their recognition

[27] Cf. *Book of the Icelanders* (*Islandica* 20 1930), pp. v–vi.
[28] *Modern Language Notes* 46 (1931), p. 487.
[29] G. A. Simcox, *Academy* (13 August 1870).
[30] *Egil's Saga*, p. 238.
[31] Stanton A. Coblentz, *New York Times* (1 February 1931).

and appreciation of both approaches to translation: Dasent's sensitive attempt at equivalence of effect, Morris's equally sensitive attempt at transmitting the experience of a scholar-poet reading the literature of a people and an age that he loved.

7

Bon-Mots from Places

'The very names of things belov'd are dear', as Robert Bridges said, and this is surely a matter of common experience.[1] Our fondness for a dog, a pub, a woman, a river, a field, a village is readily transferred to the name, so that the name not merely denotes the 'thing belov'd' but effectively connotes it and shares a place in our affections almost indistinguishable from it. And clearly we seek to give names to things with this in mind. We have a strong feeling that the name is not just an arbitrary mark for reference purposes but a fit vehicle to transmit an important part of the meaning that the object has for us. This carries with it, of course, the corollary that if it is not a 'thing belov'd' the name will correspondingly indicate that it is not dear to us. Along with Beaulieu, Lover's Lane, Fairfield, we have also the Bad Lands; and beside a field called Fillbelly, we have another called Starve-acre.

Far more than people or animals, geographical features and places of work or habitation provide special opportunity for us to bestow a name which both acts as a reference and as an indication of its meaning for us. It is natural therefore that the study of places has a widespread interest as we try to connect the place we see with the name that goes with it on the map. With many of our English place-names, making this connexion gives us little difficulty. Take Newcastle, for instance, or Southend-on-Sea, Kingsbridge, or Greenwood. The meaning of names like these is obvious, and so too the reason why they were given. In some cases—Oxford for instance—we even have the coat of arms to

[1] Broadcast as a review of A. H. Smith, *English Place-Name Elements*, when this two-volume study was published in 1956 by the Cambridge University Press.

help explain the name. Then in County Durham, even if we did not know enough about local history to realize how the new town of Peterlee got its name, we can still go and talk to the relatives and friends of the late Mr Peter Lee, and learn all about the man whose name it honours.

But with many of the older names it is not so easy. The look or sound of the name in its present-day form may be meaningless or actually misleading. By knowing what butter is, and what a mere is, we can guess that Cumberland's Buttermere was so called because the lake shores were good pasturage. And in this case we would almost certainly be right. On the other hand, Butterby in County Durham is not so easy. Many places, of course, end in -*by*, and it may not take us long to guess (and rightly too) that it means 'farmstead': Dalby 'dale farm', Mikillby 'big farm', and in the case of Butterby, well, surely, butter is a reasonable enough thing to expect from a farm. But in fact the story is very different. Originally, the place had a French name, *beu trouvé* meaning 'a beautiful find', but of course this did not mean much to people who spoke no French and the only way they could make sense of it was to assume the name must be Butterby. A similar thing happened with Beachy Head. It got its present name from Englishmen who could make nothing of the French *beu chef* 'fine headland', but who concluded, not unnaturally, that it must have something to do with the nearby seaside, 'beach'. Limehouse in London is a further example of where folk etymology (this desire to make sense out of a puzzling word) altered the earlier name. The second part of Limehouse was the same word as modern 'oast', which is still familiar to us in connexion with drying hops; but in this case it was used in the less palatable process of preparing lime in a kiln.

Folk etymology is very common even where the name is not changed in consequence. Many people know the story that connects Halifax with John the Baptist: hali 'holy', fax 'face'—'holyface'. But a far likelier explanation is that the *fax* part has only an earthy and secular reference to some kind of coarse grass. And not all coats of arms are such reliable guides as Oxford's is. The crest of the Elizabethan grammar school in Atherstone, Warwickshire, depicts an adder upon a stone, reflecting the common Elizabethan spelling of the name, adder-stone. But this is only a sort of pun and in fact the town of Atherstone has grown out of the *tūn* or farmstead belonging to an Anglo-Saxon called Aethelred, and Aethelred's *tūn* became 'Atherstone'.

It is clear, then, that we cannot rely on guesswork and the modern sound and spelling to give us the clues to the meaning of our place-names. Nor need we. The growth of historical and comparative language study from the nineteenth century onwards has put us in a much better position. We have learnt a great deal about the older forms of our language and have learnt how to interpret old spellings. This study was given an enormous boost in 1923 when the English Place-Name Society was formed under the leadership of Sir Allen Mawer, later Provost of University College London—a body which has a long association with place-name work. In the thirty-odd years of its existence, the Society has proceeded steadily with a methodical survey of the country, and a score of county treatments have been published. This has meant a patient search for early forms of names in sources such as the works of Bede, Saxon charters, the Anglo-Saxon Chronicle, Domesday Book, the volumes of the Record Commission, Rolls Series, and many others. As the names are found, they have to be identified, filed, and then interpreted by studying and comparing the earliest spellings. From the masses of material now collected, it has been possible this year [1956] for two important volumes to appear which in effect present the results of the findings so far and which show what an immense amount is now known about the way our place-names took shape. The author of these volumes is Professor A. H. Smith, the Director of the Society's survey, and he has distilled into some 750 pages both the accumulated files of the Society and his own unequalled, quarter-century's learning in place-name study.

With the help of this book it is not only possible to learn the meaning of the 13,000 place-names listed in the index—though this, one feels, is contribution enough for a book to make. The author's researches have also turned up a great deal about early English vocabulary and a lot too about the history of our people and country. We see the earliest English settlers looking upon the work of their Roman predecessors, and singling out their nobler creations with words appropriately borrowed from the Latin, *strata* and *castra*. The English form of *castra* was used in the names of dozens of the Roman townships, as we see in the endings of Colchester, Dorchester, and less recognizably perhaps in

Worcester, or Mancetter in Warwickshire. As for *strata*, we have the many places called Stratford or Stretford, Stratton or Stretton, with the element more plainly visible in Watling Street and Chester-le-Street, but thoroughly disguised in the first element of Startforth (North Riding).

Again, names like Walton, Walcot, Walworth, which appear up and down the country, remind us of another distinction that resulted from the Saxon invasion, since these names indicate pockets where the pre-English Celtic inhabitants of the country remained after a large tract of 'Britannia' had become 'England'. The element *wal-* is the same as we have in the words Wales, (Corn)wall, Welsh, and to the Anglo-Saxon it meant 'foreign, non-English', and hence it was applied in particular to those foreigners who were most in evidence, that is, their unwilling hosts and neighbours, their predecessors whom they displaced, and whose language they never learnt. There is plenty of evidence for this in place-names too; the various Pennills and Pendles, for instance. *Penn* was the Celtic word for 'hill', but it clearly meant little to the Anglo-Saxons who came upon hills so called, because they promptly added their own word *hyll* to such names. In the case of Pendle Hill in Lancashire, things were carried a stage further. When the second syllable of *Penn hyll* became obscured through lack of stress, the resulting Pennill or Pendle ceased again to have meaning and *hill* was added once more, and so the three elements of Pendle Hill mean simply *hill-hill-hill*.

Many of our place-names tell a significant story too with their reference to 'ridding' or clearing land of forest ready for tilling and occupation: names like Woodridings in Hertfordshire, Rudding in Cumberland, Redden and Woodridden in Essex, and less obvious ones like Redland in Gloucestershire, Stonereed in Kent, or Risby in the East Riding. And there is an important but complex story in the dating and distribution of the very common elements *ing*, *hām*, *tūn*, which occur for instance in such names as Reading, Shoreham, and Stapleton: it is a story of tribes, settlement, and land-enclosure.

Tribal and dialect distinctions are often indicated in the different forms a single element may take; for example, there is Coldcoats in Lancashire, Caldicott in Herefordshire, Calcott in Berkshire, Challacott in Cornwall, and Cargo Fleets in the North Riding— and all of these result from different dialect forms of the same two elements 'cold cot', which means something like 'bleak sheltering place'. The element *bōthl* 'a house' is chiefly found in the Midlands and north, but it appears as Beadlam in the North Riding and as Bootle in Lancashire, in which county it occurs also as the second part of Fordbottle and Parbold. With the element *worth*, meaning 'enclosure', we get a *three-way* regional distinction; in the north-east, parts of the Midlands, and in Surrey and Sussex, we find the simple form, as in Tamworth and Wandsworth; in the south-west this alternates with a fairly localized related form *worthig*, as in Elworthy (Somerset) or Wringworthy (Devon). Then in the west Midlands there is a third related form that results in names like Bredwardine (Herefordshire), Rigwardine (Shropshire), Bedwardine (Worcestershire).

In some cases what is ultimately the same element appears in both its English and Scandinavian forms, giving us an object lesson in the way that language differences accompanied the political ones in the days of the Danelaw. Bradford is as English as Broadstairs, *brad-* being just an early shortening of the adjective such as we find in comparing *hallow* with *holy*. But Brayford in Lincolnshire, which means the same as Bradford, indicates Scandinavian penetration, their version of the word for *broad* being *breith*. But the most obvious element distinguishing the Danelaw area from southern England is *-by*, as in Derby, Selby, Grimsby, and many others. The Vikings used this element almost exactly as the English used *tūn*, for a farmstead, and although it never ousted most of the well-established *tūn* names in the north and east, it is interesting that names in *-by* very rarely occur south of the Danelaw boundary which ran from Staffordshire to the Thames estuary.

Place-names even help us to distinguish between the two races, Danes and Norwegians, who were involved in the Scandinavian settlement. Thus the Danish word *thorp*, meaning a secondary settlement, is found chiefly in East Riding, Leicestershire, and east Midland names, indicating the Danish preponderance in the ninth-century invasions of the eastern counties. On the other hand, in the Lake District and north-west generally, we find the typically Norwegian elements like *gill* meaning 'a deep valley', as in Rossgill. These Norwegians came over to the Lake District in the tenth century from earlier settlements in Ireland, and their place-names often show Irish influence. For instance, they had picked up Irish personal names like Corc, as we see in the Cumberland place-name Corby, and even traces of Celtic word-order. Compare the regular English order of elements in the Herefordshire name Michaelchurch with Norwegian-Celtic names like Kirk Michael in the Isle of Man or Kirkandrews in Cumberland.

Even the most casual turning of Professor Smith's pages shows the variety of interest there is in place names: the indication of trades and pastimes, for instance. Hunting is referred to in dozens of names of course, while names like Bickerton (which appear in several counties) probably point to bee-keeping; Mangerton in Dorset refers to mercantile activity with the word we preserve today in *costermonger*, and *cheap* in its old sense of 'trade' is the first element in Chepstow, Chipstead, Chipley, and many similar names. Less workaday are names like Hesket or Hesketh which look back to a time when these places were noted for their race-courses, and the very popular Viking sport of horse-fighting probably lies behind both the West Riding name Follifoot, literally 'foal-fight', and also Rosewain in Cumberland, the *-wain* or *-winn* part meaning 'strife' and *hross* like *hestr* being a Scandinavian word for 'horse'. These names recall one of the most violent bloodsports, but modern taste is not likely to be much less offended by the name of one place (which I shall discreetly refrain from revealing) which in its earliest form means 'a prostitute's hovel'.

The folklore enthusiast will find that place-name study has a great deal to tell him about the customs and beliefs of the early Englishman. The name Harrow in Middlesex meant a heathen temple, and there are several places called Harrowden which like Harrow on the Hill indicate an elevated site for such shrines. Arrowfield in Worcestershire has the same element again, but with the *h* lost. Which gods were appealed to in the various temples it is hard to say, but references to Woden are particularly widespread. For instance there is Wenslow in Bedfordshire, Wensley in Derbyshire, Wednesbury and Wednesfield in Staffordshire, Woodnesborough in Kent; and by his common nickname Grim, Woden is remembered too in Grim's Dyke, Oxfordshire's Grimsbury, and elsewhere. The god whose name appears in Tuesday occurs in a few scattered places in the Midlands and South (Tuesley in Surrey, for example); and in the south only, we find a good many references to Thunor (better known to us nowadays by his Scandinavian name Thor), as in Thundridge in Hertfordshire, Thursley in Surrey, and Thundersley in Essex. A lively respect for dragons and spectres is also reflected in many place-names. The Anglo-Saxons had quite a specialized vocabulary for the various species of supernatural creatures: for instance there was *scucca* meaning a demon and *scinna* meaning a ghost, and these elements appear in the Shuckboroughs of Staffordshire and Warwickshire, and in County Durham's Shincliffe. *Pūca*, 'a goblin', whom we all know as Puck, appears in Puckeridge in Hertfordshire; he also lurks transformed (not unexpectedly from what we know of him) in Parkwells (Cornwall), Purbrook (Hampshire), and—most delightfully of all—in Poppets, Sussex. The dragon himself crops up in many names beginning with *drake*, such as Drakehill in Surrey and the various Drakelows, where the second element, -*low*, meant usually a burial mound. This -*low* part occurs in the name Taplow where indeed a remarkable burial was unearthed, full of priceless and incredibly beautiful treasure, now preserved in the British Museum. The grouping of *drake* with words meaning a hill or mound shows that the Anglo-Saxons continued to associate dragons with the traditional brooding over a treasure hoard such as we get in the Volsung story or in the Old English poem *Beowulf*. This association is especially to be seen in the name Drake North in Wiltshire—a name which has nothing to do with *north*: the earliest recorded spelling is *dracenhorde*, that is, 'dragon's treasure hoard'.

Finally, the linguist himself. There are many gaps in our knowledge of earliest English and it is unlikely that there are additional literary materials in Anglo-Saxon still remaining to be discovered which can provide us with new information on Old English words. On the other hand, there is an enormous amount still to be learnt from place names about old words long since lost and about old meanings of words. In the introduction to this new book, Professor Smith gives some tantalizing hints on how much the place-name material can fill out our knowledge of linguistic history. Hence, in fact, my title. But I fear it will seem more plausible to read into it a confession, punnily derivative from Hannah More,[2] that I am like

---

[2] From 'Florio', dedicated to Horace Walpole in 1786.

those literary cooks
Who skim the cream of others' books;
And ruin half an author's graces,
By plucking bon-mots from their places.

More plausible, perhaps, but wrong. The most cursory glance through these two learned volumes will show that the cream has not even been sampled, let alone removed: I have merely tried to indicate its richness.

8

A Commodity of Good Names

In the early 1950s a few years before his death, C. K. Ogden published a lengthy study entitled 'Word Magic'.[1] At the outset he quoted the following lines by Thomas Campbell, the poet who shares with Lord Brougham and Jeremy Bentham (and Ogden mentions this as no mere casual parenthesis) the honour of founding University College London:

> Who hath not owned with rapture-smitten frame
> The power of grace, the magic of a name?

Now of course word-magic is by no means limited to names. Strike negotiations can depend crucially on formulas—essentially linguistic: arbitrator no, mediator yes; dismissals no, redundancies yes. But Ogden is right to focus on the particular mystique of the name. A rose by any other name does *not* smell as sweet, and when we turn to names proper, *proper* names in fact—one's first name, surname, the name of home town or even surburban house—well, we don't like people to get them wrong. Some names people are not supposed to get at all. Many Orthodox Jews avoid direct reference to God, especially by the Hebrew name. The commandment against blasphemy directly reflects this. What deep-seated urge is he obeying, when a child is reluctant to tell a stranger his name? Certainly the mystical power of the name is not merely a Western or Judaeo-Christian foible. Take India for example. The original Sikh Guru, Nanak, said 'The name is the God of all gods. . . . The Sikhs worship the True Name, and thus remove all obstacles to salvation'. And Lao Tze in China, five hundred years before Christ, said of the holy man 'He saw not the things with his eyes And yet each he knew by name'—curiously similar to the power

[1] *Psyche* 18 (1952) pp. 19–95.

attributed to the Hebrew God of the Book of Psalms: 'He telleth the number of the stars and calleth them all by their names.'

These reflections were triggered off as I glanced through a book entitled *BBC Pronouncing Dictionary of British Names*, published by the Oxford University Press. Is this the first of a BBC dictionary series, I wondered? Or the final volume, rounding off such a series? Was there a BBC Dictionary of the English language or of British phrase and fable, of English quotations? Was there even a *general* pronouncing dictionary of the language? The answer to all these questions is of course 'No', so I was left with their corollary: If this was a one-off job, what was the BBC's concern for names that had made the Oxford Press's machinery burst into loud monotypical chatter? And so precise a concern: not *all* about names but just the pronunciation, and not names in *general* but just British names?

For of course name dictionaries of a more general nature are not hard to find: dictionaries of first names, surnames, place names, river names already exist, some good, some not so good, but in any case with the emphasis on history and original meaning. There are learned research projects devoted to satisfying our curiosity in these directions which will tell us how John, Giovanni, Johann, Hans, Ian, Jan, Evan, Ewan, and Ivan—all ultimately the same name—came to be differentiated in different languages; how William, Gwilym, Guillaume, Wilhelm, and Bill are similarly related; or the patronymic surnames Williamson, Williams, Wilson, Fitzwilliam, Macwilliam, and Quilliam. And that Walters, Waterson, Watts, Watson, Qualtrough form a similar set. We can learn, perhaps rather more to our surprise, that Bolinger and Pullinger are not merely the same in origin but that both are occupation names (like the less opaque name *Baker*) and both are from French, though now as remote from each other as they are from French *boulanger* which of course means a 'baker'. We can trace the similar mixture of French and English origins in our place names: *Beaulieu* obvious from its spelling if not its sound as originally 'fine place'. But who would think that *Beachy Head* began with the same element? Again, the Latin *castra* underlies not merely part of *Lancaster*, where it is fairly obvious, but also part of *Leicester* where it is not (cf pp. 112f.). The Scandinavian *bær* 'farm' underlies many Midland and North Country names like *Derby* which has the Orwellian meaning

'Animal Farm', but not *Butterby* in Durham where (as we saw on p. 111) popular reinterpretation has distorted the original *Beu Trouvé* meaning roughly 'Lucky Strike'. Celtic enclaves are remembered in the many *Waltons* up and down the country, literally 'Welsh enclosure' since to the Anglo-Saxons 'Welsh' was a generic name for the people they displaced in Britain.

It is easy to see why name study from this historical viewpoint has a widespread fascination. And not necessarily remote history. There is a fairly young name-society which sponsors the study of such sets as the proprietary names of goods, our habits in naming dogs, warships, cinemas, pubs, and suburban villas: for example, a self-consciously facetious pun (somewhat overdone) as in *Dunroamin, Dunmoving*, even *Dunkillin*, alleged to be the residence of a retired doctor. There is a launderette in the Midlands called *The Washing Well* and one in Chiswick called *Autogoin*. In all these, some general interest is obvious, as likewise in the study of pseudonyms—George Eliot, John Oliver Hobbes, Acton Bell: all nineteenth-century women novelists. Why were the Sketches by *Bez*—originally rhyming with *grows*?

The BBC volume is a different matter entirely. It is not a *study* of names at all and it is a register solely of their pronunciation, and care is taken to express the pronunciations in the scientifically precise international phonetic alphabet. It thus caters for a much narrower, recondite, even arcane range of interest in the reader, but one presumably no less keen, as the BBC is in a strong position to know—particularly that part of the BBC organization which promoted the dictionary. For the author, G. M. Miller, has for a good many years been the head of the Pronunciation Unit whose discreet but firm guidance prevents announcers and newsreaders falling into the many traps of misreading that our language—and even more, our names—confront them with. I have often been at the receiving end of calls for help from this Unit over the years, especially in the closing minutes before a news bulletin goes out, as editors find themselves confronting an unfortunate announcer with a rare word he may not know how to pronounce or with the name of a person or place that has not been in the news before. So I am aware of the meticulous trouble the Unit takes to get things right once and for all, with each item of new information filed away for future reference. They do not ring up with the same problem twice. The extent to which the general listening public is unaware of this careful pre-editing is a measure of the Unit's success: the public has developed an unquestioning trust—doubtless *too* unquestioning for our socio-linguistic health—in the unique rightness of the BBC version of a word or name.

Not surprisingly: since the BBC's conscious care in the use of English goes right back to the beginning of the BBC itself. In the early nineteen-twenties, Mr J. C. W. Reith, the young Scottish Director-General who was later to become Lord Reith, was as aware of unique responsibility as William Caxton had been at the outset of printing in the 1470s, and for a similar reason. Caxton's problem was this: Since it was impossible to print books in the form of English preferred by each buyer (as had been possible with manuscripts), what was the best form of English to adopt if one were to please a large cross-section of buyers? 'Certaynly it is harde to playse euery man, by cause of dyuersite & chaunge of langage.' Reith's problem was what form of *spoken* English was going to be acceptable for daily listening all over the country from a predominantly London-based transmitter. He set up an Advisory Committee on Spoken English which over a period of a dozen interwar years established principles which not merely gave 'BBC English' authority in the domestic and overseas services but provided a model of linguistic policy for broadcasting corporations in other countries. One reads with awe the list of distinguished people who served the BBC in this advisory role: George Bernard Shaw, Robert Bridges the then Poet Laureate, Cynthia Asquith, Rose Macaulay, Julian Huxley, Kenneth Clark (now Lord Clark), and five academics, who were, or who later became, Professors of English or phonetics: Lord David Cecil, Daniel Jones, Lloyd James, Henry Cecil Wyld, and Harold Orton.

Although in its early years the Committee ranged (and raged) over a wide field of standardization problems, its concerns (once such broad issues had been as much settled as was possible) narrowed to questions of acceptable pronunciation only, and the members were active in collecting information from all over the country on the pronunciation of names, partly personal names, but chiefly place names of England, Scotland, Wales, and Ireland.

It was natural therefore that the Advisory Committee should

E

eventually be wound up, but its work since 1939 has been continued by the Pronunciation Unit whose head has now gathered together the results of the Advisory Committee's work and greatly augmented them with supplementary data collected over the years right down to 1970.

All this goes far to explain the form and purpose of the book. It records the pronunciation of over 15,000 personal and place names of the British Isles which the BBC have had reason to file over the past forty-odd years for the guidance of their broadcasting staff. It is pointless to object that it is not exhaustive and that no very clear principles underlie the inclusions and exclusions: Wilson, Smith and Jones are in, but not Jackson, James or Johnson. A few first names are in (to tell us, for example, how to pronounce the Welsh spelling of Huw), but the vast majority are not. Most fictitious names are ignored (e.g. *Pickwick*) but some few are in (e.g. *Quatermass*), though not the name of *Kneale*, the author of *Quatermass*.

The book has 'British' in the title, and this is interpreted quite strictly. It covers names of places in or persons living in the British Isles, and if broadcasters or others of us want to know how Beethoven, Mozart, Munich, Marseilles, Haydn, or Boulogne ought to be pronounced in a British context (you will notice that this is not to question how these names should be pronounced in French or German), well, this is not our book. Similarly we look in vain for prominent American or Australian names: no Roosevelt or Arkansas, Woomera, or Canberra. One would like to say that another recent book (A. S. C. Ross's *How to Pronounce it*, published by Hamish Hamilton) satisfies our needs in this direction, but it doesn't. True, it has an entry for Boulogne (though not for Marseilles or Munich) but with an alleged pronunciation—so as to rhyme with 'you phone'—which is not to my knowledge in educated use. That example is no lonely exception. The name Arkansas (clearly the State and not the river, since Ross correctly identifies the American pronunciation) is said to be pronounced in Britain as '[ah-kan-səs], accent on second syllable', but this must surely be confined to vulgar use, by people who are dependent on the spelling.

But deciding that Ross is 'wrong' is far from being the sole ground for objecting to his recommendations, and in any case this is an area in which right and wrong are less relevant judge-

ments than right- and wrong-*headed*. Where the two books cover
the same ground, the BBC dictionary is scholarly, sound, well-
informed, and fairly complete, where Ross's—lacking the specialized and expert advisers who have been consulted at every turn
for the BBC volume—is none of these. Miss Miller enunciates
rational and fairly objective criteria for establishing the leading
pronunciation of a name. Ross is constrained by no such principles and adopts rather the stance (or Emily Posture) of a nature-
endowed omniscient. Ross of course is catering mainly for the
linguistically underprivileged and snobbery-haunted in our
midst, and it is unfortunate that these are precisely the poor souls
who are least able to recognize misinformation but who are yet
most desperately fearful of it. In this heterogeneous and highly
personal selection (by no means solely of names), Ross seems
determined to perpetuate the crudities of his U and Non-U
which in the mid-1950s achieved popularity in the worst sense
and for all the wrong reasons. It would be nice to think that his
present book is just a *jeu d'esprit* that he intends no-one to take
seriously.

Despite the limitations on what is included in the BBC dictionary, we are still left with a rich collection of names whose
pronunciation in many cases is by no means obvious even to
people who have lived all their lives in these islands: the Bysshe
of Percy Bysshe Shelley, for example, Cirencester in Gloucestershire or Jervaulx Abbey in Yorkshire. But it leaves us with especially many Scots, Welsh, and Irish names whose spelling is far
from indicative of sound, at any rate to the mere Englishman. It is
here, one feels, that the editor of this book has really gone to
town—or rather gone *from* town—to ransack bog and highland
to bring specimens before the announcer in his London studio,
otherwise insulated from all such strange sounds. Political affairs
have familiarized us with what would otherwise be the unexpected
pronunciations of Macleod or Douglas Home. But it is probably
only through a chance encounter that any of us knows how the
Welsh place name *Pwllheli* is pronounced, or the Irish family name
Geoghegan, and that the Scots family and place names variously
spelt Dalyel(l) or Dalzel(l) are in most cases pronounced more
or less as though they were spelt D'yell. Another instance of the
old letter 'yogh' being printed as 'z' (with many resultant spelling
pronunciations, as in Menzies and McKenzie) was provided as an

aside in a letter to *The Times* in April 1971 by the owner of a name more arresting than any so far mentioned, Sir Iain Moncreiffe of that Ilk; the address was given as Easter Moncreiffe and the letter was dated St Dotto's Eve. Sir Iain quotes his ancestor William as signing himself in 1558, 'Wylzam Muncreff of yt ilk wt my avn hand'.

With all such examples, however, one gets the clear impression that inclusion in the Dictionary has been influenced by the fact that a name has chanced to be required for a news bulletin at some time rather than that it presented a particular problem. 'I would to God thou and I knew', said Falstaff to Prince Hal 'where a commodity of good names were to be bought.' That is a fair description of what is to be bought in this BBC dictionary. Names in good standing, of 'good' families. Certainly where a name belongs to a famous person, the pronunciation in his particular connexion is clearly distinguished. For example, the family name *Pears* is correctly given with the two pronunciations, homophones of *piers* and *pairs*, but the editor notes which of these is used for Mr Peter Pears.

Names of people and places in the Channel Islands are listed separately in a short appendix; for the rest a single alphabetical sequence is used for the English, Scots, Welsh, Northern Irish, and Manx names. The latter are specifically mentioned in the editor's introduction, though it seems to me that Manx names are relatively thinner on the ground than those of their fellow Celts beyond the surrounding Irish Sea. Maybe this is a tribute to the Manx for staying discreetly out of the news, and we can be sure that the balance will be adjusted in a future edition if some Manx girl called Killey or Kaighin or Qualtrough becomes a public figure by having sextuplets or hijacking an airliner. Imprisonment in Ealing does wonders for a reputation.

But the topics I have been singling out for mention are all intended to suggest answers to the question of why we need a pronouncing dictionary for names. Clearly one important reason is the heterogeneity of our society and the multiple strands of its history. I doubt whether there is much demand for such a book in Portugal or Sweden, if only because racial minorities like the natives of Lapland impinge less on the life and culture of Sweden as a whole than do the Scots or Welsh on ours. Equally obviously, there has been less tradition of immigration in Portugal or

Sweden, so the question of undomesticated names like Yehudi Menuhin or George Mikes does not arise.

The matter of *history* comes up not merely because of the inter-mixture of Celt and Saxon, and the subsequent admixture of Viking and Norman, but because of the irregular relation between sound and spelling in English. There are several aspects to this question. First, it is a commonplace that the pronunciation of many ordinary words cannot be inferred from the spelling: *laughter*, *borough*, and *knowledge*, for example. Secondly, however, it is a commonplace that many ordinary words have regularized the relationship by coming to be pronounced in the way they are spelt: for example, in place of earlier *weskit* we say *waistcoat*, and instead of *forrid* most of us now say *forehead*. Thirdly, while names are no exception in either of these respects (*Thames* cannot be inferred from the spelling while a spelling pronunciation for *Daventry* has come to be used increasingly—in large measure because of the BBC in fact—in place of the earlier 'dane-tree'), spelling and sound tend to be even more acutely dissociated. One has only to recall such examples as those I gave earlier like *Macleod* and *Douglas Home*, and if it is objected that these are not English, then let us take *Holborn*, *Thames*, and *Cholmeley*. But, fourthly, not merely do names tend thus to retain an archaic spelling despite gradual change in pronunciation, but the same name can have different spellings for different families or different places. This is understandable enough when the differentiation between *Caister* and *Chester*, let us say, or between *Bury* in Lancashire and *Brough* in Yorkshire, corresponds to a difference in dialect and when the difference occurs in sound as well as spelling. But take the case of *Cholmeley* or *Cholmondeley*. There are half a dozen spellings of this name in the London phone book and the one that is least well represented—only one entry—is the spelling closest to the modern pronunciation: *Chumley*.

It may be worth mentioning another outstanding example and one with additional complications. Some people called *Feather-stonehaugh* use a pronunciation more or less corresponding to the spelling; others call themselves 'festen-haw', others again 'fear-sten-haw', yet others 'fee-sen-hay'. And then there is what Ross would claim as *the* pronunciation 'fan-shaw'. But the situation differs from *Cholm(ond)eley* in that spellings representing this least predictable pronunciation—*Fanshaw(e)*—are considerably more numerous (in the London phone directory, for example) than entries spelt *Featherstonehaugh*, and we have little justification for regarding them as variants of the 'same' name.

And although such discussions inevitably dwell on notorious instances of this kind, we must remember that variants occur just as stubbornly and unpredictably with more ordinary names. People whose surname is pronounced 'reed' or 'neel' may spell it in any of half a dozen common ways, one family clinging to one particular traditional spelling, another family sticking just as tenaciously to another.

Well, one scarcely needs to be reminded that there are very few ordinary words such as 'common nouns' in English that have variant spellings (the minor variation over a medial *e* in *judgment* is one of the rare examples), and when they do occur they are genuine alternatives—neither is more correct than another. Here we come to the really central property that distinguishes names from other words. While we may agree that the name 'Clark' may be spelt with or without an *e*, this possibility does not exist with any specific person who is actually called *Clark(e)*: his name is either the one spelling or the other, and only that one is correct. In other words, although some names are very common, the use of each one is unique in relation to the specific person or place whose name it is. The name as personal property is something which this BBC book brings out very clearly. We have already seen it in connexion with Peter Pears: his version of this spelling must sound like 'piers' or it is not 'his' name. The name that is pronounced 'bee-ment' in relation to the place in Cumberland is to be pronounced 'bow-mont' in relation to the Baroness whose title has the same spelling. Some entries are so specialized that it is made explicit that the purpose of the book is not so much to tell us how the name *X* is pronounced as how a particular Mr *X* pronounces his name. The entry *Mikes*, for example, is not for general information on this surname but for specific information on the surname of Mr George Mikes. This facet of the book's purpose is discussed in the editor's preface, a direct reflex of the BBC's policy as originally formulated by Reith's Advisory Committee on Spoken English. So far as names go, at any rate, the custom of those most concerned must prevail, correctness being relative to the specific culture, even down to the microcosm of the individual. To quote: 'It is felt that . . . the bearer of a name . . .

should be referred to by the pronunciation which he himself prefers; and that place names should be pronounced as they are locally.' A name (the Preface wisely continues) is 'a matter of vital moment to those closely and often emotively concerned with it, and unfavourable reaction to a mispronunciation . . . is immediate'. The BBC is dealing here only with sound, and the statement does not seek to put sound above spelling. I would guess that unfavourable reaction to a misspelling of our name or home town is at least as immediate as to a mispronunciation, and such is the mystic power of writing itself that the reaction is likely to be emotionally stronger.

All of which brings us back to C. K. Ogden. Commenting on the work of a scholar who was rash enough to say of the ancient Egyptians that they had an awe of names 'which is wholly foreign to western nations', Ogden lets his learned and sarcastic tongue range over what he calls the Onomancy of evangelical Christianity in our own society. 'How sweet the name of Jesus sounds', 'There is a name I love to hear', 'That one name is sufficient to lead the Christian into heights of transport that verge upon the region where the angels fly in cloudless day'. Of this last quotation, Ogden says: 'It is not the Sufi mystic Abú Sa'íd speaking, but a plain Victorian Baptist preacher.'

Both the BBC book and Ross's in effect pander to just such an awe of names, concede that a name is to be jealously protected as a piece of singularly private property having a singularly inalienable relation to the person or place to which it 'belongs'. For this reason even the objective description underlying Miss Miller's work would not have saved it from Ogden's ironic dismissal. But one might as justly (or as usefully) berate the falling leaves of autumn. Her book testifies in fact to the very power, the deep-seated, fierce unreasoning human dependence on names that he himself so caustically anatomized.[2]

[2] This is expanded from an article in *The Listener* (25 March 1971).

9

Thinking of Words

I

Words come to us so naturally that it takes a serious effort of imagination to realize what miraculous devices they are.[1] Like so many other things that are basic and elemental in our lives, we take them for granted, and we are apt to be surprised to find how hard it is to say what exactly a word is. If challenged, we might say, 'Well, words are *names* for things', and this seems fair enough at first sight. A dog is the name of a particular animal, just as William is the name of a particular man. But in fact there isn't much 'just as' about it. William is certainly the name of a particular man: we can have him in mind as we speak and could write down his address, his job, his age, something about his family, and what he looks like.

Now, recognizing William in a crowd of other men is itself a considerable feat that is not to be disparaged. We would be hard put to it to explain just what the features are that make us pick him out without hesitation where, to people who do not know him, he really looks very similar to a great many other men. But we need to realize that this ability is quite unlike—in fact almost diametrically opposed to—the feat we perform when we recognize *a dog* as such. In this case, the 'particular' animal, dog, is an indefinitely large class of animals, whose members can be physically very different from each other. Our eyes are now not looking for the unique features of William but are carefully ignoring unique features, looking beyond them for a quite abstract generalization. It requires no great imagination, in fact, to suppose that someone from a different planet might well see greater similarity between a pekingese and a cat, than between the peke and an Irish wolfhound or a great dane; between an afghan or an

[1] Much of the material in this chapter was broadcast as a series of short talks in the summer of 1973.

Old English sheep dog and a Shetland pony, than between the afghan and a peke.

In short, our word *dog* entails a stupendous feat of generalization and abstraction, an effort that allows us to disregard very obvious differences and to take instantaneous account of only certain basic similarities that are by no means obvious. And we must not think that *dog* is an awkward special case: it is absolutely typical. We find an exactly analogous situation with the objects that we group as *doors*. If we look around the kitchen, we see there is a door into the hall, perhaps another into the dining room; there are cupboard doors; the oven has a door that perhaps opens downwards; there may be a sliding door beneath the sink unit; the china may be in a dresser with a glass door. Yet the similarly framed glass above the sink which opens similarly on hinges, is not a door at all, but a window. If we try to write down just what a door is, so as to include all the things that any five-year-old will call a door, and exclude all the things such as lids and windows that neither we nor he will call a door, the extreme difficulty will give a sobering insight into the power of abstraction we operate with these simple everyday words. And we may look on the five-year-old with renewed wonder.

And so far we have talked only of nouns, and of so-called concrete nouns at that. Consider how much more remarkable is the abstraction and generalization involved in using such a word as *pity*. Here we are a step further from the notion of William as the name of a man. If it was hard to imagine how we abstract what is common in all breeds of dog so as to exclude big cats and little ponies, there was at least (we may have thought) a set of physical objects which in the last analysis we could line up and whose physical, visible properties we could compare. But *pity*? How do we learn the range of feeling that this covers? How do we learn to distinguish between pity and love and sorrow and sympathy and remorse and charity and regret? How do we come to know that these words are relevant for us even to group with pity, instead of (say) with anger?

Well, of course, there are those who say we can never really know what other people mean when they use these familiar words; that we have difficulty enough in knowing what we mean ourselves. Is the sorrow that we feel, for example, at a death, pity for the person no longer able to enjoy life? Sympathy for the family bereaved of a loved one? Is it personal regret over the loss to ourselves? And when an acquaintance says he did something 'out of charity', do we not sometimes wonder whether this means out of selfless love or just out of a sense of duty that he perhaps grudges?

In our heart of hearts, however, we know that there is usually no need to be so cynical. We are confident that most of the time most of the people mean the same as we do when we use even these abstract words like *sympathy*. We scarcely realize how utterly miraculous this is, and we certainly do not usually realize how lucky we are who share the miracle equally. What about the unfortunate minority who have no equal share? It is difficult and painful to imagine what it would be like if we could not under-stand what people meant by a door; if we did not know the difference between a door and a window, pity and love. The panic-stricken disorientation can perhaps be simulated to a very slight degree in what happens when we drive into a patch of fog. How quickly we lose our bearings, our sense of direction, our ability to recognize simple objects now that they are partially masked. Can we not begin to have some inkling of the enraged terror enflaming that languageless autistic child next door?

II

It is often said that, provided we are not of the unfortunate minority of people who have pathological language defects, our language mechanism automatically equips us to say anything we need to say. This does not mean that I can talk about all the technicalities of company law or of central heating with the glib-ness of a solicitor or a plumber. What it does mean is that if my job or my hobby entailed a knowledge of these activities, my language would rise to the occasion. It is rather like Parkinson's law. There is a natural linguistic ecology which dictates that our 'stock of words' expands or contracts according to the demands made on it. As the horse-drawn carriages declined in use, so we lost the need and hence the ability to refer to the differences which eighty years ago were freely expressed by words like phaeton, brougham, or landau. But of course we have balanced such losses with words which distinguish between convertibles, fastbacks, dormobiles, and minibuses.

We thus have the general truth that any normal person has the language tools to handle anything he needs to handle. But there are odd little exceptions. Let us consider, for instance, forms of address to strangers. Quite often we need to draw a person's attention to something that has just dropped out of pocket or handbag, or to the fact that he is just going to walk into a plate glass door. Not merely does English lack anything corresponding to the French *attention* or German *Achtung*, but we do not have the equivalent of *M'sieur* or *Madame* or even *Mademoiselle*. Some people manage very effectively with 'Watch it, mate' or 'Look out, lady' or even 'Hey, missis'; but these forms are outside the range of polite educated usage. We can try shouting 'Excuse me!', but that is ambiguous: it may be taken to mean that we just want to push past in a hurry. 'Excuse me, *sir*' is awkward unless you are a very young male speaking to a much older one. 'Excuse me, *madam*' makes you sound like a door-to-door salesman—and can hardly be addressed to a teenage female in any case. By this time, the stranger has bumped into the plate glass, or has disappeared, leaving you to take a fur glove to the police station.

Not long ago, a foreign visitor whose English is extremely good told me of his embarrassment in a tea shop. He knew that although we can call out 'Waiter' to a man, we cannot call out 'Waitress' if the place is staffed by women. So he tried *Miss*, and had been forced to cringe by the large middle-aged married waitress who had turned on him: 'And who are you calling *miss*, young feller?'

There are many such arbitrary little limitations on our language. While we can single out one story or one yarn from a number of stories, we can't talk about 'a news' or 'an information'. Instead, we have to use a roundabout expression like 'I have another piece of news (or another item of information) for you'. While underclothes (informally, undies) are made up of individual garments, we can not complain to the laundry that they have mislaid one 'underclo(the)' or one 'undy'. While we can talk about *John's car* or *Mary's car*, or *John and Mary's car* if it belongs to the two of them, we are in difficulty if one of the possessives is a pronoun: *John and her car*. A friend of mine recently slipped into saying *This is Mary and I's car*. We can ask a person how many children he has without going into the specifics of whether they are boys or girls; but we can not ask him how many brothers and sisters he has without getting precisely these irrelevant sub-answers and then totalling them.

Now, it is true that in this instance we may use the word *siblings*. But the very fact that this word is mainly confined to technical health-authority usage (despite our recognition of its usefulness and of our need for such a word) is an interesting indication of the way we are very largely the helpless prisoners of the language in general use around us. We like to think that we make our language as we need it, but in fact the scope for an individual to change things is very limited. Even where there would be widespread agreement that there is a linguistic deficiency, very few communities in the world seem to have settled the means whereby remedies can be agreed upon and adopted.[2]

Let me touch upon one other way in which we are equipped somewhat less than ideally to say what we want to say. I mean the problem of 'word-finding'. Let us pretend that we are writing something or—worse—that we are in the middle of a conversation, and we want to refer to what goes on when people are doing something together in full knowledge of each other's motives but seem unwilling to disclose those motives to others, perhaps because their activity is harmful to other people's interests. We may turn over in our minds some such long-winded paraphrase of what we want to say and even at the end not feel satisfied that the paraphrase has in it all that we mean. Yet we may remain convinced that a single word exists which says exactly what we have in mind. *Collaboration, plotting, co-operation, conspiracy, partnership*: we fish around and reject each of these in turn because they either say too much or not enough. It is worrying when we can not find the right word, and it is worrying too that when we find it—in this case, *collusion*—it has no obvious relation to the rough paraphrase we started with: it is not as if the word turned out to be 'selfish-secret-work-together'. Finally it is worrying that when we are struggling to find the 'right' word in this way, there is no certain or systematic way of setting about it, and no guarantee either that the word exists or that if it does we will inevitably find it.

Can we not begin to imagine how near to despair these people must come who can almost never find the word they are hunting for?

[2] Cf. V. Tauli, *Introduction to a Theory of Language Planning* (Uppsala 1968).

Our feeling of helplessness when we cannot find the right word, even when—as we say—it is on the tip of our tongue, gives us some insight into the lonely and terrifying impotence of the person who through serious language disorder is regularly and chronically in this position.

In the spring of 1969, four government ministers, under the leadership of the Secretary of State for Education and Science, made me the chairman of an inquiry into the speech therapy services of England, Scotland, and Wales.[3] And so, in the three or four years that followed, I saw a good deal of the linguistically disabled—and of the dedicated overworked profession that is solely responsible for tending to their needs: the speech therapists. The scale of the problem alone makes it seem utterly intractable. There are somewhere in the region of three hundred thousand sufferers—men, women, and children, scattered throughout every part of the country, and attended by only about the equivalent of eight hundred full-time speech therapists, struggling manfully (womanfully rather: there are virtually no men in the profession) against hopeless odds of isolation, regional scatter, poor facilities, and overwork.

Eight hundred therapists to three hundred thousand patients does not of course mean an average case-load of three or four hundred patients for each therapist. What it means is that many sufferers have to endure impossibly long periods on waiting lists with no treatment at all. And every month the waiting lists get longer. The proportion of our population linguistically disabled is actually increasing, as a result of three major factors. First, the greatly improved post-natal care now available gives the 'at risk' births a better chance of survival. Secondly, greater longevity in the population at large produces more geriatric speech problems. Thirdly, there is—as a result for example of industrial and road accidents—an increase in the kind of head injury that entails linguistic disability.

But the size of the problem is no more daunting than the range. There is a bewildering variety of impairments, many of them

---

[3] The Report of the Committee of Inquiry was published by HMSO as *Speech Therapy Services* (London 1972).

intricately connected with other mental and physical disorders, and many of them very little understood. The poor GP, whose training has all but ignored the complex human language mechanism, often cannot even detect—let alone diagnose— a language disorder. A sufferer may thus, at the crucial time, miss the chance of being referred to a speech therapist who alone has had relevant training for attempting to tackle these complex disabilities. The stammerers and those with defects of physical structure such as cleft palate can be thought fortunate by comparison with those who entirely lose the power to utter words through laryngectomy. And since the disabled in these categories may at least understand language and thus be fully in one-way communication with those around them, they are in turn better off than those who through brain lesion from a road accident or a cerebral thrombosis have partially or entirely lost their ability to understand human language or to produce anything better than nonsensical strings themselves.

One can see in such patients the extremes of distress in word-finding that we can palely imagine with our trivial everyday difficulties in getting the word (*co-operation*? *collaboration*? ah, *collusion*) that is on 'the tip of our tongue'. I remember being with a therapist who was attending to the problems of a former teacher, aged about forty-five, once highly verbal and articulate, now depressed and humiliated and confused by his isolation and perhaps by a frightening disorientation in which dogs and cats, doors and windows, regret and pity had lost their definition, the comforting crisp identity that language had once given them.

But the patients whose plight is most distressing are the children with delayed or defective language development—conditions that are commoner in little boys than in little girls, and in families which have already less than their fair share of health, happiness, and security. Where they cannot get treatment that is both timely and adequate, one can see them (as Baroness Brooke said in the House of Lords in December 1972) 'turn in on themselves in self-defence or from despair'. And even with speech therapy and a happy home atmosphere of speech stimulation, the unfortunate aphasic child is delayed in his schooling, with educational, emotional, and ultimately economic consequences whose seriousness cannot easily be exaggerated.

When you think of the powerful and well-organized dental

services, devoted to helping people *chew*, it is quite devastating to reflect how little our society has done to build up and sustain the profession whose job it is to help people *talk*, and so participate in man's most important attribute: his ability to use words.

IV

Our bookshops and libraries are full of books on the use of words, on the English language, for all ages and educational levels. Why? we may wonder. After all, the normal child learns to talk as naturally as he learns to walk. I am applying the same two words, *learn* and *naturally*, to these two activities quite deliberately. 'Learn' because with talking as with walking we see the child obviously making efforts to acquire skill, sometimes failing, sometimes succeeding, as he takes his first steps, an expression we can apply metaphorically to his talking as we can apply it literally to his walking. He appears to imitate adults and older children, weeps when he fails, crows when he succeeds. And we say 'He's learning fast!' So the use of *learn* with both talking and walking seems obviously appropriate.

But the word 'naturally' is equally applicable. We do not *teach* a child to walk or talk: he learns how to do these complex activities himself. Of course, we offer a helping hand: again literally in the case of walking. We pick a child up when he has fallen; we hold his hand when he is trying to walk over a rough or slippery surface; we may remove objects from his path when he is toddling across a room. We may provide him with devices like a wheeled frame which will stimulate or facilitate his efforts. But we do not teach him to walk in the sense of telling or showing him what to do, as we will teach him to drive a car fifteen years or so later.

So too with talking. We encourage the child; we stimulate his own talking by ourselves talking to him; we gently correct a word here, supply a word there; we answer his unending questions; we help enlarge his stock of words and help perfect his pronunciation. But we are aware somehow that we are not so much teaching him to talk as observing how fast he is learning to talk; by his own efforts, as it were. Naturally.

This of course is part of the difficulty we run into with 'English' as a school subject. What is the English teacher supposed to be teaching? Well, hardly to *speak* English as the French teacher has to teach English children to speak French. The English children probably speak better English before the English lessons start than their French teacher speaks the French he teaches.

Well, there is in fact plenty of English for the teacher to teach. If it is natural for children to talk and there is little the teacher has to do beyond continue the stimulation the home environment has begun, it is by no means natural for children to read or write. There is no community in the world—in whatever backward state of development—in which the children do not talk their local language with the same eager competence that our own children have in English. But of course there are plenty of communities in which only a tiny minority of people ever learn to read or write—and indeed it was only a minority of our own countrymen who could do so until relatively recently. So the complicated job of getting the naturally-acquired language skills of *ear* and *tongue* transferred to the *eye* and pen-clutching *fingers* has to be done through the educational process.

We begin to see some of the reasons why so natural an activity as using words has to be supported by a daunting array of books about words. But books to teach reading and writing are only a small part of the array. The two central types of book about words that we expect to find are dictionaries and grammars, and they are flanked by many others, less structured and more discursive. There are books about the history of words—where our words came from, how they came to have their present meaning, how Shakespeare or Chaucer or King Alfred used words differently from what we find usual today. I suspect, however, that many who read such books are not primarily motivated to find out how Shakespeare or Chaucer spoke, but are concerned rather to find out more about the nature of language itself.

I have talked to many different kinds of audience beside university students: women's institutes, townswomen's guilds, trade union groups, miners' lodges, even prison audiences. And I have never yet failed to find anything but the keenest interest in what might well seem quite useless pieces of information. Like this: We say that a person is *frank* (i.e. 'open') ultimately because about 1,500 years ago, when the Franks conquered what is now France, they made themselves the only *free* men in that multiracial area. *Chivalry* originally had to do with horses, and we admire it because our forefathers admired the knights who were able to go

round on horseback. *Sabotage* gets its reputation from the damage
that a worker wearing clogs or sabots could do to property by
kicking it. Such fragments serve as attempts to probe—hardly to
explain—a human facility which, though completely natural and
manifestly central to the wellbeing of individual and community,
is also an abiding mystery. The popularity of books about words
testifies to the popular awareness of this mystery and to the almost
universal urge to know something more about it.

V

Of all the books about words, the type that springs most readily
to mind is the *dictionary*. It used to be said that if a home contained
any books at all, the two you could depend on finding were the
Bible and a dictionary. Whether or not the ubiquity of the Bible
still holds in what are sometimes called these post-Christian days,
the widespread ownership of a dictionary certainly does.

There is more to our language than just words, but the classic
word-book—the dictionary—seems to many people to be the
receptacle for the whole language, indeed to be the symbol of it.
There seems to be something comforting about having on one's
bookshelf a handy directory to all the words of the language. For
that is what we seem to regard the dictionary as being (cf. Chapter
11 below).

Let us glance at one fairly commonplace example of the com-
fortable reliance we place on dictionaries. In the game of scrabble,
it is usual for the players to take the nearest available dictionary
as the standard for admissible words. If a player forms a sequence
of letters we are dubious about, we seize the dictionary, and if our
suspicions are confirmed, we can say in aggrieved triumph,
'There's no such word!'—and our opponent has to retreat in the
face of this unchallengeable evidence.

It is worth considering some of the implications of this. First,
there is the assumption that, although we are all free to make up
new sentences—in fact even though we *expect* every sentence we
hear to have been constructed for that specific occasion—there
are severe constraints on the individual making up new *words* as
he goes along. Secondly, and despite this, there is the overt
acknowledgment that, however fluent and educated and well-
read he is, no native speaker is expected to know all the words of

his language. We must ignore on the present occasion the first of these two implications, but perhaps we can think a little about the second.

It is strange in a way, surely, that, although he learns his native language very early (so that by the age of five he can use words like *dog* and *door*, *love* and *fear* and *hate* and *hunger* quite correctly and effortlessly), an educated man in his fifties should still be able to say, 'I'm afraid I don't really know what such-and-such a word means; I'd better look it up in a dictionary.' There are at least two important reasons for this. Words are the indices of experience, and since we are liable—if we are active or lucky—to go on encountering entirely new experiences from the cradle to the grave, we shall equally go on learning the words that refer to such new experiences. It might not occur to us that our educated middle-aged man could still have anything to learn about English four-letter words, but if he is a solicitor or a shopkeeper, he may well have never moved in yachting circles and so find himself ignorant of the noun *yawl* or the still shorter navigational verb, *yaw*.

This is readily paralleled among speakers of other languages, but the second reason probably affects speakers of English especially. It is the fact that English has basically two types of word—the familiar homely-sounding and typically very short words like *cat*, *king*, *crazy*, and *kiss*, and the more learned, foreign-sounding and characteristically rather long words like *corrugated*, *carbolic*, *catechism*, and *chrysanthemum*. There are far more words of this latter type among the half-million words of English than of the former type, and it is chiefly these that we start learning relatively late in our use of English, and go on learning (and maybe forgetting) throughout the rest of our lives. One reason why we may not have come across a particular one of these before, in fact, is that many of them have meanings for which we have alternative and simpler expressions. 'I don't like arguing with him: he *prevaricates*', we hear someone say—and we may wonder what *prevaricate* means without realizing that it is more or less what we have long used the verb *quibble* for.

Again, a man may be forgiven if he does not know what is meant by the question 'Is Mrs Jones *primiparous*?'—though he would have understood perfectly well if the doctor had asked whether she was having her first baby. And even when we have frequently encountered and used such words as *convex* and *concave*, we may continue to have difficulty in remembering which is which and be fearful of using either. Shakespeare was among the first to illustrate (see Chapter 3 above) how easily impressed we are by the opaque 'hard words' we see and hear around us. More than one school authority is said to have scared off trespassers with such notices as 'Beware of Wild Oxymoron and Anacoluthon'. An enterprising menagerie proprietor is reported to have prevented customers from lingering on his premises with an attractive sign that read: 'This Way to the Egress'.

Such issues can hardly arise in a language with a relatively homogeneous lexicon such as German has. Although like *primiparous*, 'erstmalig gebärend' is chiefly in formal medical use, its meaning is quite transparent to any German speaker. This may mean that we need dictionaries more than Germans do: at any rate, it probably makes them more interesting to use.

VI

Not long ago a numbered resident of one of Her Majesty's prisons wrote asking me to unscramble for him the difference between participles and gerunds. And it is not only people with—dare I say—time on their hands who show a keen interest in such quite technical aspects of language. People notice that superficial similarities conceal profound differences, as with

> His *wife* is cooking the dinner
> His *job* is cooking the dinner

People notice potential ambiguities in syntactic structure as with

> We hung out red and blue flags

(were some flags red and others blue, or was each flag parti-coloured?) Many of us are amused by grammatical acrobatics such as those in which Anthony Burgess is especially skilled: 'He had breathed on me, bafflingly (for no banquet would serve, because of the known redolence of onions, onions) onions.' Writers tease their readers with sentences that make them aware of multiple structures. This is particularly easy with partial parody. The witticism *Familiarity breeds* cannot be understood simply as 'Children are conceived when folk get too familiar with each other'; we cannot dispense with a reading which compares the entirely different structure in the proverb on which it is based, 'Familiarity breeds contempt'. So too in Saul Bellow's *Herzog*, the multiple parody of 'A bitch in time breeds contempt' has only one correct reading for the novel ('A bitchy woman eventually gets despised') but we are entertainingly obliged to match this against the different grammar of the two proverbs which exist for us outside the novel.

Here is where books about grammar come in. Grammars and dictionaries are the two chief types of books about words, but whereas dictionaries are concerned mainly with the meaning of individual words, grammars are concerned with the way we construct phrases and sentences by stringing words together. Sometimes we use a grammar book for an explanation of puzzles and ambiguities that interest us, such as the examples we have been considering. But sometimes we use a grammar because we are doubtful about what is the acceptable form of a sentence we want to construct. Should we write different *from*, different *than* or different *to*? Should we compare one thing *to* another or *with* another? Is it all right to say 'I was *that* tired, I fell asleep' or should it be '*so* tired'? May we write 'Everyone should do their best' or would it be better to have '*his* best' or even '*his or her* best'?

Now it so happens that, as native speakers, we would scarcely be capable of *asking* such questions if we did not know perfectly well that rules of entirely different kinds are involved here. On the one hand, one or other of the variants we question 'feels' perfectly natural and would be the one we would all tend to use if we were not afraid of being criticized for linguistic bad behaviour. On the other hand, we are aware of a form which comes less naturally, but which we know or suspect is preferred by some people or in some styles and varieties of English. In such instances, our grammar book becomes a manual of style, a sort of linguistic Emily Post book, explaining and discussing the basis of preference according to the situation we find ourselves in—familiar conversation (in which case, whichever form seems most natural is probably the best to use), all the way along the spectrum of usage to writing a solemn or formal document (at which point, convention may demand an expression which seems anything but natural to most of us).[4]

[4] See further R. Quirk and S. Greenbaum, *A University Grammar of English* (London 1973), Ch. 1.

Clearly, the sort of information we seek from grammars (or from dictionaries for that matter), where these are concerned with our own native language, is quite different from the information we seek from the grammars or dictionaries of a language we have learnt at school or university. The most important function of the books about our own language is not to give us essential guidance that we need before we can open our mouths. Rather, they educate us in the nature of language itself. They help us see the relation between language on the one hand and thought and experience on the other. They can explain the social and stylistic indices that are inextricably tied up with linguistic expression: so that when someone speaks, we not merely listen out for what he means, but also for what his way of saying it has to tell us about his attitude to us, perhaps also where he comes from, and what sort of education he had. In short, these books help us with the questions that seem to arise naturally and perennially in people's minds from the unending interest and mystery of 'mere' words.

VII

Man is a rational, reasoning animal so why can we not have a strictly logical language? And when we see clearly how illogical our language is, why can we not agree to change it? In one form or other, this question is one that frequently comes up in letters from members of the public. I remember being told what a condemnation of our attitudes it was that we classed all books as *fiction* and *non-fiction*—thus relegating all the serious, factual, learned writing to the negative status of not being novels and stories. Why (my correspondent demanded) should we not regard non-fiction as central, call it perhaps *faction*, and then refer to novels and the like as *non-faction*? Certainly, our use of words tends to betray, whether we like it or not, a particular orientation or attitude to what lies behind them. Grass is a weed in a flower bed but not in a lawn. We can readily sympathize with the visitor to Spain who, when asked if she was a foreigner, said 'Certainly not: I'm British.'

A letter from Cumberland brings up a different aspect of the odd ways that words have. The writer pointed out that we say 'in the *realm* of fancy', 'in the *sphere* of politics', 'in the *field* of mathematics' where, although *realm*, *sphere*, and *field* in such usages mean more or less the same thing (which is wasteful), they sound wrong if they are interchanged ('in the realm of mathematics', for example), which is illogical.

Then there is the hardy annual about number and gender with pronouns like *everybody*: 'Anyone can lose their way, can't they?' Since *anyone* could be a man or a woman, it is argued that strictly we should say 'Anyone can lose *his or her* way, can't *he or she*?' —but thank goodness, no one does. To avoid the feeling that *they* (being plural) is ungrammatical with reference to 'anyone', people sometimes settle for *he*: 'Anyone can lose *his* way, can't *he*?' but this raises fresh difficulties, since to the literal-minded this seems to exclude women, and to the liberal-minded it seems to slight them. It was to get out of this quandary that, in approving the draft of a bye-law, a local authority is said to have added the ambiguous rider: 'The Council wishes to make it clear that *man* regularly embraces *woman*.'

Only a few months ago, someone in South Africa wrote to ask my advice and assistance in getting acceptance for some quite far-reaching changes in English that would remove some features that women's lib supporters object to in our language. The proposal was to abolish sex—at least so far as pronouns are concerned. For example, instead of having to distinguish linguistically between *him* and *her*, we should refer to both as *het*. 'Everybody must do *hets* best'.

But the realities of linguistic life are stubborn. Whether we think some or all of these suggestions are silly, or whether we think some or all of them are highly desirable, it is very doubtful whether we could carry out any change. Even in those countries that have official language academies, it is more usual to find the academy describing and explaining changes that have taken place than successfully decreeing changes that *shall* take place. Human language reacts poorly to logical or even democratic decisions, even in a country that prides itself on logic and a revolutionary spirit: 1789 and all that has not abolished *m'sieurs et mesdames*, and despite the distinguished precedents set by presidents, a French audience would collapse in scornful mirth if I began a lecture with 'Français et Françaises!'

So too, although some official bodies—especially in the United States—dutifully use the new emancipated title 'Ms' in place of both *Miss* and *Mrs*, it is doubtful whether there has been any change at the point where virtually all linguistic activity takes place—on the tongues of ordinary people. In all such matters, we confront deeply-engrained natural habits that can not be changed at the whim of passing political fashion. While many gender-free words exist (in English *cousin, family, relative, friend,* for example), it seems at least equally natural, and certainly at least equally widespread, to reflect sex differences in languages, and also—as the Council put it—to make men embrace women.[5] This is as true for *homo, maðr, l'homme* as it is for English *man.* The extensive series like *god-goddess,* German *Freund-Freundin,* French *cousin-cousine,* Polish *Pan-Pana* show furthermore a tendency (which can not by definition be other than natural) to define the female in terms of the male, and although we may delore this, as we may deplore classifying history and philosophy as *non*-fiction, it is quite another matter to change it.

Language does of course change, is always changing, and with the advantage of hindsight we can often explain *why* a change took place. But it is not quite so easy to plot the stages and processes by which a change actually took place, and until this aspect is fully understood, there is little possibility of going on to the still obscurer matter of *making* a change take place. I hope we shall eventually get to this point, but if and when we do, the first priority will not be to stop classifying history as non-fiction or even to start abolishing sex-referring pronouns. A far greater need will be to use our skill to defuse the linguistic bombs in places where men, women, and children hate each other (and even kill each other) in the name of no higher ideal than the Tower of Babel, no grander cause than the confusion of tongues.

[5] On this issue of 'unmarked' terms having inclusive meaning, cf. R. Quirk and A. H. Smith, *The Teaching of English* (London 1964), pp. 29 ff.

10

Third International

Dictionaries have come a long way since Robert Cawdrey gathered two or three thousand words together and published in 1604 his *Table Alphabeticall of Hard Words* which could be fitted into little more than 100 pages. Now, 'for the price of an overcoat' (as the blurb tells us), we are offered this magnificent and meticulously complete register of English vocabulary with nearly half a million entries: *Webster's Third New International Dictionary* (1961), edited by Philip Gove.[1] The fact that its nearest British rival, the *Shorter Oxford English Dictionary* of about the same scale and coverage, can be bought for a third of the money (the price of a sportscoat, if the choice must be sartorial) should not diminish our admiration for this Merriam-Webster achievement and its many palpable advantages over any other dictionary in existence.

Prominent among these is its very genuine newness. Soon after its predecessor appeared in 1934, the editorial staff set about collecting material on a massive scale, and four and a half million slips were assembled recording modern usage. As a result, the definitions in the present edition ('Every line of it is new,' says Dr Gove) rest squarely upon reputable documentation which is as up-to-date as dictionary material can possibly be. This means that we find relatively new words like *turbo-prop* and *radar* not merely included but splendidly defined; a *beatnik* is 'a person having a predilection for unconventional behaviour and dress and often a preoccupation with exotic philosophizing and self-expression'. One only regrets that the editor does not follow the practice of other scholarly dictionaries and chance his arm to the extent of revealing the dates of his earliest recorded references.

Just as important as new words, and far more difficult for the

[1] This review appeared in the *New Statesman* (2 March 1962).

lexicographer to detect, are the new uses of words which have a long history in the language—and a long tradition of dictionary treatment. The new Webster earns good marks on this account too. *Thesaurus* is recorded in the 'Roget' sense (ignored by most dictionaries), and—more impressively—*anthropoid* is recognized as having in addition to the traditional sense, 'man-like', the more recent sense, 'ape-like', which has resulted from the frequency with which the word is collocated with *ape*. (If anyone doubts that this sense is genuine, he has only to try the experiment of telling a friend he looks rather anthropoid and then, as the firework labels say, standing well clear.) What is more, the copious files have enabled the editor to illustrate particular uses of words on a lavish scale from contemporary writers. Mr Alistair Cooke, for instance, is quoted as using *monstrous* in the sense of 'very great'. Many of these quotations have little more than curiosity value, it is true, but they provide valuable reassurance that they are not merely *illustrations* of uses but represent the raw material on which the editorial staff have based the description of these uses.

The newness of the *Third New International* (the first *New International* appeared in 1911) is not in question, then, though by no means 'every line' of the pictorial illustrations is as 'new' as the lines of type. The block illustrating coracles has appeared before—and looks it: and it seems unnecessary to perpetuate the image of the tulip-shaped telephone. But these are small matters when the illustrations on the whole are so excellent and so welcome. What of the 'International' aspect? We on this side of the Atlantic are in a glass-house situation if we criticize an American dictionary for paying scant attention to extra-American usage. Indeed, it was in part the neglect by British lexicographers to deal properly with American English (a neglect which is still too common) that spurred Noah Webster to write a dictionary of American English for Americans. But of course there were more powerful factors: the Declaration of Independence meant for Webster, as for Adams, Jefferson, and Franklin, linguistic as well as political independence. The one was even regarded (as so often in national movements) as a condition of the other. Webster's lexicography was understandably rather pugnaciously American, therefore, and in consequence it is understandable too that the linear descendants of his dictionaries (as the Merriam-Websters alone are) should find it more difficult than some other American dictionaries to nurture a fully international editorial policy. The long list of actual staff is naturally enough uniformly American, but it is surprising that even of the 200 'Outside Consultants' there appears to be only one non-American specialist, this being a British lady whose responsibility was limited to the field described as 'Girl Guiding'. Little of the three and a half million dollars spent on the dictionary would seem to have gone on off-shore contracts.

It is true that the coverage of specifically British and Commonwealth words is fairly good (*windscreen, trafficator, roundabout*, and the like), but the editor seems not to have grasped that for international use it is equally necessary to label as American the words and uses that are restricted in this way too. The entry for 'telephone box' very properly states that this expression is British: but the entry for 'pay station' (which is accompanied by a line-block illustration of a telephone box) carries no hint of a comparable restriction. And even American readers might find it useful to be warned that *nudnick* is not universally used by English-speaking peoples for 'a person who is a bore'. Indeed, is this word subject to no social or stylistic restraints in America? Apparently not—or at any rate none describable in the dictionary's scheme of usage labels, which admits a category 'slang' but not 'colloquial' or 'informal'. Such a lack of refinement is rather regrettable. In the *American College Dictionary* of Clarence Barnhart, two uses of *awful* are distinguished as 'colloquial': the senses 'ugly' (as in 'an awful hat') and 'very great' (as in 'an awful lot'). In the new Webster, four or five times as extensive, no such distinctions are made and these two senses are put on the same footing as the sense 'inspiring awe' (as in 'an awful majesty'). On the international aspect, one might just add one's regret (but not surprise) that pronunciation continues to be indicated with so little regard to the long-established conventions of the International Phonetic Association. And incidentally, how widely valid is the pronunciation of *monster* and *spinster* (but not *minster*) with a medial 'z'?

American dictionaries (like British ones in earlier times) have an attractively encyclopedic tradition. In the present instance there are fine colour illustrations covering a wide variety of subjects from Manx cats to colour itself: indeed, the article on colour is an excellent example of the American dictionary tradition at its best—an authoritative and detailed account of spectrography, with several tables and diagrams, and complete with references to recent discussions in the learned journals. And of course this degree of scholarly detail is to be found equally in articles dealing with other fields of study. Unlike many American dictionaries, however, Dr Gove's work does not register persons and places as such. He has in fact reduced the size of the book by about 500 pages as compared with the last edition, and while this has been achieved partly by typographical changes (which he mentions), another important factor (which he does not mention) has been the dropping of proper names. In the 1957 edition of the *Second*, for example, there was an entry for New Zealand (describing it as 'a British colony'!); now proper names are recorded only insofar as they have an attributive use. In which case, by the way, they are entered for some obscure reason with lower-case initials: *new zealand, united states.* (The lists of Editorial Assistants and Consultants do not record the co-operation of mr e. e. cummings.)

The publication of the new Webster is a major event in the lexicography of English, and one cannot do justice to a large and noble book of this kind in a short review. Perhaps the fairest epitome would be that it is difficult to imagine in so compact a form so vast, so authoritative, and so up-to-date a body of information on what Dr Gove describes as 'the most important language on earth'. But one last point: those who intend to forego that overcoat would be well advised to order the two-volume edition. The weight and mercurial suppleness of nearly 3,000 pages within one cover will sorely try even the elegantly sturdy binding that Messrs Bell have provided.

II

The Image of the Dictionary

It is hazardous to embark on topics as enmeshed in folklore as the influence of the dictionary or Anglo-American differences; to embark on both simultaneously is little short of foolhardy.[1] There is a widespread belief that the dictionary exerts more influence in English-speaking societies than elsewhere, and like other widespread beliefs there may be something in it. But it is easier to hypothesize on the reasons (our very large and mixed romance, classical, and native vocabulary; our irregular spelling, etc.) than it is to substantiate the premise. There is also a widespread belief that the dictionary's Diktat is more insistent and more obeyed in the United States, and again it is easier to find plausible explanations than it is to find solid foundations for the claim. It may be true that the educational and social systems in America create a predisposition for dictionary power, and I have no answer to Uriel Weinreich's rhetorical question, 'Where else do high-school teachers of the native language work to instill in their pupils "the dictionary habit"?'[2] But predisposition does not inevitably trigger off results, and just because high-schools work to instill habits, it does not follow that the habits get instilled.

I am of course merely pleading for more objective evidence rather than venturing to deny the folkloristic beliefs. And indeed a good deal of evidence transcending mere anecdote exists already of the totemic relation of the dictionary to American society. Consider the outburst over the Webster Third, reminding us of the way Uzzah, the son of Abinadab, was struck down for

[1] This paper was presented at the International Lexicography Conference, New York Academy of Sciences, June 1972.

[2] U. L. Weinreich, 'Lexicographic Description in Descriptive Semantics', in F. W. Householder and S. Saporta, eds., *Problems in Lexicography* (Bloomington, Indiana 1962), p. 27.

laying his hands on the Ark of the Lord: Dr Gove nearly suffered the same fate for laying his hands on the sacred book that we might call Noah's Ark. The story of Uzzah is told in what the Authorized Version calls one of the Books of Samuel, and this may serve to remind us that the Pax Britannica has never been analogously disturbed by a feeling of sacrilege perpetrated against any of the books that have sprung directly or indirectly from the loins of Samuel Johnson.

Doubtless the dictionary has indeed less symbolic or emotional power in the UK than in America, but if so it is a matter of degree and not of kind; and the difference should not be exaggerated. In Britain too it seems that the dictionary is the language's bible and its only bible. It is the recourse of the faithful protestant who is able thereby to prove—for example—that 'there is no such word'. There is the same twist to the opening of St John, with the belief that In the Beginning was, not the Word, but the Dictionary. *The* dictionary, of course, not *a* dictionary: just as you can buy bibles of different sizes and in different bindings, so dictionaries can look different but they are just different editions of *the* dictionary. And if all this is just a sarcastic academic allegation,[3] it is no more an allegation for Britain than for America.

More seriously, for some 350 years dictionaries have had two outstanding emblematic values in Britain. First, as repositories of information and truth. The metaphor 'a walking dictionary' for a supremely well-informed person is used identically by Shakespeare's contemporary George Chapman:

> And let a scholar all Earth's volumes carry
> He will be but a walking dictionary

and the late Victorian F. C. Selous who wrote of one man that he was 'a perfect walking dictionary concerning all matters connected with . . . South Africa' (*Travels and Adventure*). Second, as museums for rare and curious specimens of language. Another of Shakespeare's contemporaries has the Doctor in *The Duchess of Malfi* name a 'very pestilent disease' as *lycanthropia* which the Marquis of Pescara greets with 'What's that? I need a dictionary to 't', as he would not presumably if the doctor had spoken of wolfish inclinations. In *Sartor Resartus* (1831), Carlyle comments

[3] Cf. T. Pyles and J. Algeo, *English: An Introduction to Language* (New York 1970), p. 123.

on one who calls 'things by their mere dictionary names', and with reference to Carlyle's own style, George Meredith forty years later (*Beauchamp's Career*) wrote of the rough-and-tumble mixture of 'street-slang' and 'learned dictionary words'. Whether or not the common words are in a dictionary, one thinks of a dictionary as typically containing the hard and rare ones. It is not just spouting lots of words but lots of *long* words that makes us say 'He's swallowed a dictionary'.

But we are still in the realm of folklore and anecdote. A quotation, whether by or about Carlyle, need have no universal application. In an attempt to acquire information more general, more factual and more modern, I prepared a questionnaire on monolingual English dictionaries and induced an interesting sample of British youth to respond to it.

SUBJECTS: Two hundred and twenty subjects, selected both for homogeneity and range, submitted themselves to the questionnaire. The *homogeneous* factors are as follows: all were native English-speaking British; educated in the British Isles; undergraduate students at University College London; half way through the first year of their studies in the academic year 1971–2. In respect of *range*, half of the subjects were students in the 'humanities', and half in the 'sciences'. In both cases, 'pure' and 'applied' studies were well represented: two-thirds of the humanities students were in the 'pure' fields of history, philosophy, and English, one-third in the 'applied' field of law; one-third of the science students were in the 'pure' fields of chemistry and biochemistry, two-thirds in the 'applied' field of medicine. The subjects were roughly half men and half women.

QUESTIONNAIRE: The questionnaire consisted of thirty items summarized as follows, retaining the original numbering and order, but omitting the items which served only as a check on the subjects' personal history, field of study, etc.:

(2) When the subject last used a dictionary
(3) Average frequency of use
(5) Concern to consult a particular dictionary
(6) The dictionary normally consulted
(7) Subject's ownership of a dictionary

(9) Knowledge of both British and American dictionaries and basis of preference if any

(10) Ownership and use of dictionary in parental home

(11) Subject's reason for most recent use of a dictionary

(12) Subject's most usual reasons for use

(13) Subject's failure to find what he wanted

(14) Subject's suggestions for improving a dictionary

(15) Should citations be from named (and well-established) authors?

(16) Comprehensibility of definitions

(17) Adequacy of definitions in respect of subject's own knowledge

(18) Use of a dictionary for pronunciation

(19) Adequacy and comprehensibility of pronunciation symbols

(20) Use of a dictionary for form-class information

(21) Should dictionaries be complete, even with well-known words like *throw*?

(22) Should dictionaries have encyclopedic entries?

(23) Use of a dictionary for etymology

(24) Should dictionaries contain American English words?

(25) Should dictionaries contain slang words?

(26) Use of a dictionary for synonyms and antonyms

(27) Adequacy of a dictionary for finding synonyms and antonyms

(28) Should dictionaries contain regional dialect words?

(29) Should dictionaries contain phrases and idioms (like *take your time*)?

(30) Subject's further suggestions for improving a dictionary

RESULTS:

The responses to each question were considered in relation to several parameters of obvious possible relevance—for example, the subject's field of study—and attention was paid to whether in this connexion it might be more appropriate to consider his specific subject (e.g. philosophy) or the broader field ('humanities') or with a cross-classificatory orientation ('pure'). In some cases, responses themselves yielded parameters in relation to which other sets of responses could usefully be considered. This turned out to be the case, for example, with item 3 and it was found relevant to consider subjects in relation to the average frequency with which they consulted a dictionary: 'weekly', 'monthly', or 'infrequently' (this last including everything from 'every couple of months' to 'virtually never'). Subjects' responses to other questions were then scrutinized in relation to each individual's frequency of dictionary use. Where statistically significant or suggestive co-occurrence of factors was observed, this will be noted below.[4] Commonly, however, responses showed no such co-occurrence and in such cases the results may be taken as representative of the British student population as a whole, with the obviously important implications that spring from this observation.

Ownership of a dictionary (item 7). For example, of the 220 subjects, 192 were found to possess a dictionary of their own, and this majority represented all students equally, irrespective of field:

	Humanities	Science
Owning	97	95
Not owning	15	13

There was some tendency, however, for ownership to correspond with regularity of use, and this, though perhaps not as strong a tendency as one might expect, was statistically significant:

	Owning	Not owning	
Monthly (or more frequent) use	145	11	
Infrequent use	47	17	$(p < .001)$

Experience of deficiency (13). On the other hand, while no clear majority emerged from the subjects as a whole in response to the question whether they remembered being let down on consulting a dictionary, there was in this instance a significant difference between groups of subjects. Those in 'pure' studies, whether humanistic or scientific, were proportionately much more aware of having failed to find what they were seeking than those in the 'applied' fields of law and medicine:

	Pure	Applied	
Dictionary found deficient	80	48	
Dictionary not found deficient	32	60	$(p < .001)$

[4] Chi-square tests were done on all the numerical data, and where these revealed significance at least as strong as the 5 per cent level ($p < .05$), the probability is shown as a fraction of unity. I am grateful to Mrs Hilary McKeon for help in scoring the subjects' responses and to Mr T. Leonard for statistical advice and calculation.

To judge from subjects' comments, this should probably be taken to imply a more critical use of the dictionary by students in 'pure' fields rather than that dictionaries were necessarily less well informed in some subjects (e.g. philosophy) than in others (e.g. law).

Users' discrimination (5). Certainly, while there was a two-to-one majority of 'indiscriminate' users, critical acumen varied according to academic interest on the question of whether subjects were particular as to which dictionary they used on any occasion:

	All	Humanities	Science	
Discriminating	70	51	19	
Not discriminating	150	61	89	$(p < .001)$

But in this case there turns out to be a correlation not only with field of study but with frequency of dictionary use. The 'dictionary habit' appears to go with a tendency to discriminate in the selection of dictionaries:

		Humanities	Science	
Weekly	Discriminating	29	9	
users	Not discriminating	23	13	
Monthly	Discriminating	15	6	
users	Not discriminating	21	40	$(p < .005)$
Infrequent	Discriminating	7	4	
users	Not discriminating	17	36	$(p = .05)$

This comes out more clearly perhaps in a simplified table:

	Weekly users	Not weekly users	
Discriminating	38	32	
Not discriminating	36	114	$(p < .001)$

Frequency of use (2, 3). As to frequency of use itself, there was a wide range within all groups of subjects, but a clear tendency for students in the humanities to make heavier use of a dictionary:

	Humanities	Science	
Weekly	52	22	
Monthly	36	46	
Infrequently	24	40	$(p < .001)$

Reasons for dictionary use (10, 11, 12). Here too there was a wide range of response among all groups of subjects, but the most striking feature is the difference between (*a*) the *subjects' own use* of dictionaries and (*b*) their impression of the use to which dictionaries are put in *the parental home*. Subjects were not constrained to name only one use and on the other hand a minority did not volunteer any at all. Nevertheless, while information on the meaning of words is clearly dominant, it is easy to see the wide spread of functions in the home situation as compared with the heavily study-oriented use among the subjects themselves:

	Meanings	*Spellings*	*Word-games*	*Other uses*
(*a*) Subjects	149	58	15	29
(*b*) Parental home	82	38	57	41

The 'other uses' are highly miscellaneous and their chief interest perhaps lies in the evidence they offer that some of the dictionary features which seem of particular centrality to lexicographers are decidedly peripheral to the ordinary user:

	Word finding (e.g. synonyms)	*Ety-mology*	*Usage (e.g. averse to/ from)*	*Pronun-ciation*	*General interest*	*Children's homework*
(*a*) Subjects	11	7	4	2	5	—
(*b*) Parental home	1	2	9	5	4	20

The last two columns here, of course, do not necessarily (or even probably) imply additional types of information sought but rather specific categories of motivation for seeking information. And an additional motivation for possessing a dictionary was offered by one subject: its value as a 'status symbol'. This was of course a sport response statistically, and doubtless meant in sport as well, but it is perhaps significant that the idea should have crossed the subject's mind, even in jest.

In respect to their own use, the two predominant needs—for meanings and spellings—seemed to be felt generally throughout the various groups of subjects. There was some tendency, however, for spelling to crop up more frequently among the responses of science students; and with respect to meaning there was specific reference to the need for precise and technical definition among the students of philosophy, law, and medicine. The use of a technical dictionary was however mentioned only once.

After the items eliciting in this way the various uses of a dictionary that occurred spontaneously to subjects, the questionnaire directed the subjects' attention to certain specific uses. On item 26, *word-finding* (e.g. synonyms and antonyms), there was strong and widespread interest, 156 subjects saying they often used or tried to use a dictionary for this purpose, and only 62 saying they did not. Perhaps some of the latter were influenced by the difficulty of using a dictionary successfully for word-finding; 140 subjects had experienced such difficulty (item 27) and only 49 had found dictionaries adequate in this respect.

Much less interest was expressed in *etymology* (23) and other historical aspects of words, 121 subjects reporting that they never sought such data; this was particularly common among the science students:

	Humanities	*Science*	
Used for etymology	56	30	
Not used for etymology	49	72	$(p < .001)$

Lack of interest was also common among the subjects who made infrequent use of dictionaries for any purpose. Nevertheless, a strong minority of 86 said that interest in etymology was a frequent reason for using the dictionary, a view understandably common among those students of English who were inclined to be dictionary addicts.

There was still less general interest in *pronunciation* (18), 139 disclaiming dictionary use in this connection. The minority of 62 who wanted information on pronunciation were again strongly associated numerically with those who were frequent users of dictionaries:

	Weekly users	*Not weekly users*	
Wanting pronunciation	28	34	
Not wanting pronunciation	38	101	$(p < .025)$

It is unlikely that the general disinclination was aggravated by difficulty in understanding the system for indicating pronunciation (19), since only a slim majority of 115 out of 220 seemed to experience any such difficulty. Nevertheless it is of interest that those with difficulty tend to be those who have least acquired the 'dictionary habit':

	Weekly users	Not weekly users	
Finding difficulty	29	86	
Not finding difficulty	39	50	$(p = ·005)$

As to *parts of speech* (20), only a small number of subjects, 27, said they were in the habit of looking up words to get information on form class, while 190 subjects disclaimed any interest in this matter. Even so, there was a significant difference between groups of subjects:

	Humanities	Science	
Use for parts of speech	20	7	
No use for parts of speech	91	99	$(p < ·025)$

The dictionary 'image'

But perhaps a general disavowal of specific interest should not influence lexicographers to drop certain features from future editions. In the group of questions which sought to establish what the general image of a dictionary was in the minds of the subjects, the criterion of absolute completeness, for example, was strongly supported. This was true even where (item 21) the question implied that the inclusion of the very common words and meanings increased the cost of production (and subjects commented critically elsewhere on the high price of dictionaries). Yet only 53 voted for the omission of the 'easy' matter, a minority that tended to be especially small among the humanities subjects and among the frequent users:

	Humanities	Science
Favouring omission	21	32
Not favouring omission	90	74

	Weekly users	Not weekly users	
Favouring omission	7	46	
Not favouring omission	66	98	$(p < ·001)$

A similar result was obtained for item 29 which referred specifically to common idioms (like *'take your time'*) and which put the question the other way round: Should these be included? The answer was 'yes' by 145 to 72.

But completeness, further investigated, is defined by close and conventional limits. Responses to items 25 and 28 showed that there must be no slang (142 to 70) and no dialect (147 to 61). By a narrow margin (and only a narrow margin), American English is put in neither of these classes and escapes the exclusion fiat (24).[5] But the result is equivocal and, against those who feel that it is scientists who have their eyes and ears most open to America, the results showed a greater readiness to include American English items on the part of the humanities subjects:

	All	*Humanities*	*Science*	
Include Am. Eng.	114	68	46	
Not include Am. Eng.	102	40	62	($p < .005$)

But if American English is just 'in', this does not apply to another aspect of potential completeness: encyclopedic entries such as 'Freud, Sigmund' (22). Though British dictionaries have sporadically appeared with such features for centuries, and there are noteworthy present-day examples, they are rejected by 123 to 96, the numbers being spread fairly evenly throughout the groups of subjects.

All of this adds up to a fairly complete 'identikit' constituting the general image of '*the*' dictionary in the minds of British students, irrespective of their academic interest. The dictionary is a *definition-specifying* register of the *linguistic* or *generic* (as opposed to the proper) words of the *national* (as opposed to regional) *standard* (as opposed to slang) language. It seems likely that it is the socio-political aspect in '*national* language,' rather than specifically anti-American undertone, that produces the deep division over the principle of whether it is right for a dictionary to be 'Amphi-Atlantic'. And as far as the standardness of the language is concerned, the user is prepared to trust the lexicographer.[6] On item 15, subjects rejected by 132 to 84 the idea that meaning and usage should be attested by quotations from named and established authors, a feeling significantly stronger among science students:

	Humanities	*Science*	
Identified citations	50	34	
No identified citations	60	72	($p < .05$)

[5] Cf. A. W. Read, 'The Labelling of National and Regional Variation', in Householder and Saporta, eds., *Problems in Lexicography*, pp. 221 f.

[6] Cf. L. Zgusta, *Manual of Lexicography* (The Hague 1971), p. 292.

Indeed, among the humanities students who are also dictionary-addicted there was a slight converse preference:

	Humanities only	
	Weekly users	Not weekly users
Identified citations	26	24
No identified citations	24	36

This concept of the dictionary corresponds closely, of course, to the Concise Oxford which probably plays a large part in sustaining such an image even if it has not actually created it. Examples are editorial; *Freudian* and *Froebelism* are in but not Freud or Froebel; American English items are prefixed by a warning asterisk (an unhappy emblem when we consider what a starred form means in linguistics).

Scrutinizing the responses to items 6, 9, and 10 showed that the subjects (all but 28 of whom possessed dictionaries of their own and all but 7 of whom came from dictionary-owning homes) drew their experience of dictionaries for the most part from the Oxford family. Only 33 subjects claimed any acquaintance with American dictionaries and only two of these confessed to having in consequence acquired a taste for them (one of these in any case saying grudgingly only 'for some things'—unspecified). If there is 'proof that American dictionaries are now supreme',[7] UK students seem lamentably unaware of it. In the parental homes there were 133 dictionaries of the Oxford family (mainly the *Concise* and the *Shorter*) to 97 others; the 97 included 12 dictionaries of American provenance and numerous non-Oxford British ones, but since it also included 26 subjects who could not remember the identity of the parental dictionary, it is very likely that the true result would still further swell the Oxford set. It is noteworthy that, where the students' preference for their own use is concerned, the Oxford proportion rises to 161 as compared with 51 others. See Appendix I, pp. 161f.

Deficiencies

Although, as we have seen, meaning and definition are of central importance to most subjects, there is considerable dissatisfaction over the dictionary's contribution in these respects. An overwhelming majority of university students apparently experience difficulty in understanding the metalanguage in which definition is expressed (item 16). But as with the peripheral interest, pro-

[7] A. Isaacs, 'Dictionaries and the Scientist', *New Scientist* (5 March 1970).

nunciation, so with this central interest, difficulty with the metalanguage is associated with the unfamiliarity that proceeds from infrequent dictionary use:

	Weekly users	Not weekly users
Difficulty with definitions	49	113
No difficulty	24	32

It is also (and independently) associated with field of study, scientists having proportionately greater difficulty:

	Humanities	Science	
Difficulty with definitions	72	90	
No difficulty	40	18	($p < 005$)

In more detail and bringing in both parameters, the responses are distributed as follows:

		Humanities	Science	
Weekly users	Difficulty	31	18	
	No difficulty	21	4	($p < 05$)
Monthly users	Difficulty	25	40	
	No difficulty	11	6	
Infrequent users	Difficulty	16	32	
	No difficulty	8	8	

Still stronger dissatisfaction was expressed about the adequacy of definitions (17), no less than 175 of the 220 subjects having found from time to time that they knew more about the meaning of a word they were looking up than the lexicographer apparently did. Of the science students, there were especially few who had not had this experience:

	Humanities	Science	
Definitions inadequate	81	94	
Definitions adequate	31	14	($p < 01$)

Suggestions for improvement

Halfway through the questionnaire (14) and again at the end (30), subjects were given the opportunity to jot down ideas they might have on improving the dictionary. The response was striking in several respects but notably (*a*) the fertile interest in making suggestions, well over two-thirds of the subjects contributing;

(*b*) the fact that subjects in all groups were equally keen to suggest improvements; and (*c*) the widespread agreement (corresponding to the consensus over deficiencies that we have already noted) on the major points, again irrespective of the subjects' academic field. See Appendix II, pp. 162f.

There was greatest concentration of suggestions in three main areas: *definition*, *coverage*, and *layout*. On the first of these, 52 subjects had points to make: most of them considered that definition should be made less complicated, opaque, and lengthy; and almost a half felt that definition should be made less general and imprecise. As expressed, the dissatisfaction suggested a certain degree of contradictory recommendation, some subjects feeling that definitions could be made clearer if they were made *more* general and that part of the muddling impression they now give resulted from the lexicographer's inability to capture a 'wide' meaning within which the fragments would assume a relatable shape. It is likely that the contradiction is only apparent, however, masking an underlying agreement on sources of dissatisfaction.

On the second area, coverage, 38 subjects made suggestions. There was a general anxiety that dictionaries should be updated more efficiently, that they should be not merely more modern but more colloquial, and that they should strive for comprehensiveness and accurate detail.

On the third area, layout, 36 subjects had observations to make, the two predominant ones being (*a*) that with the help of better typography and less cramped arrangement dictionaries would be more easily readable, and (*b*) that systems of cross-reference and better symbols could make dictionaries more efficient.

It is difficult to imagine so many young people from diverse fields of interest joining enthusiastically to produce so many well-conceived ideas for improving any other class of book than a dictionary. This is itself a strongly suggestive index of the important place that the dictionary possesses in our society. When we further consider the degree of confluence and congruity in the ideas offered and of the agreement in responding to the other items in the questionnaire, albeit with significant differences according to subjects' academic interests, we recognize that it is not just a matter of how important is the place of the dictionary but of how institutionalized and uniform is the image of the dictionary in our society.

Appendix I

Item 6: *Dictionaries normally consulted by students*

Oxford: 161
- COD — 63
- POD — 32
- SOD — 22
- Illustrated — 3
- OED — 6
- Etymological — 2
- Unspecified — 33

Collins	13
Chambers	12
Penguin	7
Cassell	6
Roget	2
Blackies	2
Webster	2
NED (John Bull ed. 1926)	1
Penguin Science	1
Funk and Wagnall	1
Nuttalls	1
Elizabethan	1
Readers Digest	1
Cambridge ?	1

Item 10: *Dictionaries in parental home*

Oxford: 133
- COD — 42
- SOD — 32
- POD — 16
- Illustrated — 4
- Unspecified — 39

Name not recalled	26
Chambers	21
Collins	13
Cassells	10
Webster	5
Nuttalls	4
Readers Digest	4
Funk and Wagnall	3
Universal	2

Odhams	2
Blackie	1
Harrap	1
Larousse	1
Elizabethan	1
Routledge	1
Cambridge ?	1
NED 1952	1

It should be noted that rare items occurring in both lists reflect a general tendency in the responses for students to prefer the same dictionary as that reported in the parental home.

Appendix II

Ideas on the improvement of dictionaries made in response to items 14 and 30. The number of subjects associated with each suggestion is given except in some cases where a point was made by only one.

(A) *Definition.*
  (*a*) General need for clarity, 32, comprising:

less complicated or unclear	16
less lengthy	5
less repetitious	2
less circular	3
less detailed and fragmented	2 ⎫ (but cf. A *b*)
less general—aim at 'wide' meaning	4 ⎭

  (*b*) Need for less general and imprecise treatment (scientific words, for example, are poorly treated with certain uses not covered), 13.
  (*c*) Other points:
      give more explanation and fewer synonyms, 2;
      give more pictorial support, 2;
      clarify definition by outlining semantic history, with dates, 3 (cf. B).
(B) *Etymology.* Fuller treatment required, 13 (more research needed on history of English; dictionaries 'should have an etymological section'; explain how words are derived, 2).
(C) *Coverage* needs to be more modern and more comprehensive, 38, comprising:
      more modern material, 15 (newly-coined words, 3; modern

idioms, 2; modern words, 5; more orientation towards modern society, 1; need constant updating, 4, so as to 'play a part in preserving all facets of the language', but let a loose-leaf accretion system remove need for buying whole new dictionary too often: cf. J).

more colloquial material, 8 (more colloquial, 1; more slang, 3; lighter material, 1; more idioms, 1; less formal material, 2).

more comprehensive and detailed, 13 (of whom 7 specified need for more technical words, e.g. of law, biology, science (but cf. G); 2 mentioned that dictionaries were too limited in the type and amount of material covered; even cheap dictionaries should contain the more obscure words) (but cf. F)

a dictionary should have a good abbreviations section, 1; and should 'list the Greek and Arabic alphabets', 1.

(D) *Encyclopedic entries* required, 4 (but cf. F, J).

(E) *Thesaurus material* and orientation required, 13 (7 specified synonyms, 2 antonyms, and 2 suggested a combined dictionary and thesaurus).

(F) *Less comprehensiveness* should be the aim, 4 (too much information, 1; simple words and meanings unnecessary, 3).

(G) *Specialized dictionaries* required, as separate books to meet separate and specialized needs, 4.

(H) *Usage and examples* should be better treated, 7 ('usage in context', 2; more concrete textual material, 4; have verse and prose examples, 'like Johnson', 1).

(I) *Pronunciation treatment* needs improvement, 4 (in better system, 3; easier to understand, 'like Penguin').

(J) *Lay-out* should be improved, 36, comprising:

less cramped presentation, 11 (bigger print, 2; fewer abbreviations, 4; better spacing, less compact);

better printing, 2 (better type face);

sectional arrangement, 3 (cf. C, E, G): separate parts for etymology and definition; loose leaf for accretion of addenda;

easier reference, 14 (comprising 5 who wanted more cross-references and 2 who wanted less; 2 wanted to know how one found a word without knowing the spelling—a not unreasonable *cri* in view of *chameleon* or even *ghost*; 3 wanted a simpler reference system (without 'Greek symbols', 1); 1 wanted an index treating words like *make* which 'have different meanings according to context'—?idioms; 1 wanted cross-reference to an encyclopedia for treatment of appropriate items: cf. D).

(K) *Computerization needed.* 1 (without further explanation).

(L) *Price* should be lower, 5 ('Why not a large paperback?').

12

Our Knowledge of English

Not long ago I spent a couple of weeks in and around the hills and woods of eastern Belgium, and with the luxury for once of some time to think, I not unnaturally thought of Sir Lacon Threlford to whose memory this paper is dedicated.[1] It seemed to me increasingly natural that, with his close ties with the Cercle Belge and the Anglo-Belgian Union, he should have presided also over the Institute of Linguists. I moved, fascinated, from village to village where bilingualness is a powerful if not dominating linguistic and social fact, and where within a few miles one hears the Frankish Mitteldeutsch in Aachen and out towards Bonn and Cologne; Dutch to the north-west; French to the south; while in Belgium we find an interlocking maze of Flemish and French speakers, and in Luxembourg the use of French, German, and Letzeburgesch. Not only is this whole area full of profound interest for linguists, but here the people themselves are for good or ill acutely confronted with the sober knowledge of the social power of language and with the need to acquire knowledge of languages far beyond the experience or even consciousness of the vast majority of people living in the English-speaking countries. And I found myself reflecting on the significance of what has often been noticed: that it is to linguists in the small countries of western Europe that we must still turn for an analytic knowledge even of our own English language—above all to the Dutchmen Poutsma and Kruisinga, and to Jespersen the Dane. It is well known, of course, that the learner of a foreign language, even if he never acquires native-like mastery, has in some respects a grasp of its structure which he can make explicit much more

[1] This was the Threlford Memorial Lecture delivered to the Institute of Linguists at the British Academy, 19 November 1966.

readily than can a native speaker; but it seems significant that it is in those countries where second language learning is part of the whole environment that we find a higher than normal proportion of scholars engaged in scientific language study.

Among the insights that Jespersen had, we may mention the comments on certain adverb uses that he made in a Society for Pure English Tract in 1937 entitled, 'Linguistic Self-Criticism' and to which he returns in the notes for the final volume of his *Modern English Grammar*, posthumously published in 1949. He observed that it made a radical difference whether these adverbs appeared before or after the verb—as in 'He naturally replied' and 'He replied naturally', and that whereas in the second instance the adverb relates to the manner of his replying, the first 'implies a judgment on the part of the speaker'.[2] Thus, 'He naturally replied' means 'He replied, as seems to me perfectly natural'. Now, of course, every native speaker has always known this, insofar as we have always used the two positions for the adverb consistently and unhesitatingly in this way. But it is quite a different kind of knowing that enables us to formulate what contrast is involved and how it is achieved. Indeed, we are still a very long way from understanding all the rules for adverb usage in English and the language bristles with other difficulties too, which as native speakers we find it hard even to notice.

Consider, on the one hand, sequences of adjective plus noun: *a pretty girl, a useless object, an intelligent dog*; the relationships here are not merely clear to us all, they also are regular and symmetrical: the girl *is* pretty, the object *is* useless, the dog *is* intelligent. Now consider the superficially similar sequences of noun plus noun which are equally clear to us but which are far from symmetrical and which conceal a bewildering array of relationships that have never yet been fully explicated. A *sherry bottle* is a bottle that contains sherry, but a *glass bottle* is a bottle which is made of glass. A *récord player* is a device that plays records but a *record pláyer* is a person who achieves records in his playing. A *house boat* is a boat which has some of the properties of a house, but a *boat house* is a building where boats are kept. A *bedroom* is a room which contains beds, a *dining room* is a room for dining in, and *headroom* has to do with vertical measurement, while *head man* denotes a man who is the head or chief. A *factory hand* is a worker in a factory

[2] *Modern English Grammar* (London 1949), VII.2.65.

(singular) but a *factory act* prescribes regulations about factories (plural). A *corkscrew* screws out corks, and a *pickpocket* picks things from pockets. And so one could go one. 'Idioms', we are tempted to say, with individual and arbitrary meanings, each sequence an isolated phenomenon. But this is not true, as we can easily test by considering some sequences which we are not likely to have heard before. We find ourselves able to assign meanings to them, indeed, often impelled to assign unique meanings to them, even if such meanings amount to nonsense. *Service station* is in French *la station service*, but if we used 'station service' in English it would neither mean 'service station' nor yet be meaningless: it would mean 'the kind of service you get at a station', a notion suggestive of desiccated sandwiches and not a porter to be found. Beside *wine glass*, 'glass wine' would mean wine made from glass: beside *factory hand*, a 'hand factory' would be a factory that manufactured hands; beside *corkscrew*, a 'screw cork' would be a stopper that could be screwed in; beside *pickpocket*, a 'pocket pick' would be a pick that could be carried in one's pocket. So far from being relegated to the area of idioms or to the province of the lexicographer, noun-noun sequences are thus seen to manifest regular grammatical patterns, an integral part of what Noam Chomsky has called the 'competence' of the English speaker, however elusive these patterns are to describe and formalize.

Nor need we go so far from what is ordinarily thought of as grammar, in order to demonstrate the point that it is difficult for the native speaker to know how much he knows about his own language or his own use of it. Ask a man about his use of *who* and *whom*, to take a very hackneyed point on which people are as linguistically conscious as they are on anything. It is unlikely that he can tell you much and still less likely that he can be accurate in what he tells you. He may tell you stiffly that he always uses the two forms 'correctly' and leave it at that. He may be the devil-may-care type who says he never uses *whom* and always uses *who* where less brave souls cling to *whom*, yet he is in fact more likely to say, *Who did you see* than *The man who I saw*, and he is very unlikely ever to be heard saying *The man to who I spoke*. One would be equally unable to elicit from one's neighbour—or, indeed, oneself—whether it was usual to say *He didn't dare go, He dared not go, He didn't dare to go*, or *He dare not go*, and there ought to be a big award for anyone who can describe exactly what makes him say 'I started to work' on one occasion and 'I started working' on another.

Now it was this paradoxical inaccessibility of well-assimilated linguistic habits that moved us at University College London some years ago to institute the Survey of English Usage. Not only were we concerned to make explicit the facts of everyday usage: we sought also to investigate the extent to which an individual's selection of grammatical form varied as between speaking and writing, informal and formal occasion, specialized and non-specialized material. But since English had been subjected to examination by grammarians for three hundred years and since the last fifty years had seen the mammoth compendia by Poutsma, Kruisinga, and Jespersen, it is necessary to ask why this new look at English was necessary, and in what ways the new look would, in fact, be new. For all their excellence, which in many ways we could never equal let alone surpass, the big grammars fell short in our view for two main reasons. In the first place, their generally eclectic use of source materials too often leaves unclear the distinction between normal and relatively abnormal structures and the conditions for selecting the latter. In the second place, not surprisingly in view of the absence till recently of easy recording devices, the major descriptions of English leave us largely in the dark about the forms used in spoken English.

Having said why we thought a new look was necessary, let us turn to the ways in which our procedure has developed and the ways in which we hope we are producing new information. Central to the entire operation is the notion of assembling for analysis a large corpus of English as it is actually used, a corpus that is reasonably representative of the repertoire of educated professional men and women in their activities, public and private, at work and at leisure, writing and speaking. By basing our description on such a range of actual usage we have sought to avoid both of the deficiencies in older descriptions that I have mentioned. But, of course, no corpus, however large, could be expected to give information in the requisite degree of detail on all the grammatical structures of English. Indeed, it is difficult to conceive of a body of texts large enough to inform us fully even on inflexional variations such as I mentioned earlier in relation to the verb *to dare*. We have, therefore, additionally developed psycholinguistic techniques to investigate the native English speaker's potential performance, to catalogue items in his linguistic repertoire that do not necessarily emerge in the actual instances of usage that an observer may assemble. Finally, it is necessary to develop procedures for analysis: that is, techniques for handling vast quantities of data and tracing the regularities and their co-occurrent features of language or occasion. In this connexion, the advent of the electronic computer in recent years has opened up possibilities for analysis with a degree of sophistication beyond the wildest hopes of linguists in earlier generations.

The main components of the Survey thus baldly outlined are illustrated in the accompanying figure, and we may now describe their nature in a little more detail.

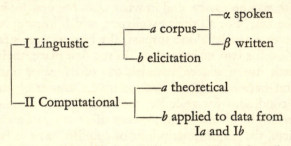

First of all, whose English is it that we wish to describe? I have already mentioned this as being the English of 'educated' men and women. This is a shorthand characteristic of the people who write books, who lead our cultural, educational, political, and religious life, who constitute the major centre of imitation in language, in the sense that it is these people's English that is thought to be best by society as a whole, these people's English that is taught to foreign learners, and so on. The concept is not an easy one to formulate, though in fact there is broad agreement on it. And, since there are probably more of such people who are educated to university-level than not, and since the number of people educated to this standard is adequately large, we take this level as our cut-off point in choosing samples of English for inclusion in our corpus.

I spoke also of making this corpus 'reasonably representative of the repertoire' of educated people—'reasonably', be it noted, not 'statistically' representative. Since all of us probably use

English predominantly for speaking not writing, and for speaking to our family and friends, a truly statistical sample would contain only a trivially small amount of material other than spontaneous colloquial speech. We have thought it better to be guided by the consensus of informed opinion on this matter, and thus a group of us with experience of studying varieties of English (people, that is, who had had the opportunity of forming a view as to where important linguistic differences lay in the uses of English) agreed upon a text allocation after consultation. The pooling of ideas in this way gave us both the categories of English that we think it important to recognize and also the proportion of material to be collected in each category. Thus, in spoken English we have four main categories: conversation, spontaneous commentary, spontaneous oration, and prepared oration, each with sub-categories, but the first of these we regard as most important and threequarters of our spoken texts will lie in this area, which is divided into conversation between intimates, between equals, and between disparate participants. Cutting across this categorization is another, a circumstantial classification, according as the material was collected surreptitiously, or in the known presence of a microphone, or over the telephone. Again, conversation is further subdivided as between business and social matters. The basis of the typology is now probably clear enough without my needing to describe the other subclasses in spoken English.

Turning to written material, we have recognized three major classes, each with several subclasses. Most important is printed material to which we devote three-fifths of our text allocation. Within this class we distinguish learned writing (subdivided between artistic and physical studies), instructional writing (that is, popular arts—the 'how to do it' books), general non-fiction (such as biography, travel), printed news, administrative and official language, statutory language, persuasive writing (as in essays and sermons, for example), and finally prose fiction. Our second major category is manuscript and typewritten material, with chief subdivisions into letters, continuous composition, and private journals (including those written for ultimate publication). Finally, there is the class of material which takes shape originally in the written medium, but which is written in order to be heard—drama especially, of course, but also radio talks and news.

I have used the word 'text' several times. This is a technical term in the Survey, being the unit in terms of which the corpus is measured. A text is a stretch of language 5,000 words in extent, whether we encounter the language from which a text is excerpted in print or manuscript or in natural speech. It thus makes it easier for us to keep the necessary control over the amount we excerpt from any one author, but its importance goes far beyond this. The Survey's analysis is different from earlier grammatical inquiries in not merely searching textual material for examples of specific constructions: we insist on the need to account for every structure, be it common or rare, in every text of our corpus. This is the most valuable constraint I know upon the temptation that affects every investigator to wish his preconceptions and pet theories upon the data he is describing.

Now, even a corpus of two hundred texts (a million words) will not present a complete picture of English usage or anything like it. This is a point already made above. With the corpus as the foundation of our description, we have to look further for rare constructions and to find other than textual means to investigate the influences operating on a speaker to produce even the common ones. Our chief technique in eliciting linguistic information has been described in a recent book by a colleague and myself, and only a few words on the main principles involved need be said on the present occasion. Let us assume that we want to know which negative preterite form of *dare* is preferred by someone, and whether he likes and would himself use the sentence *He would have liked to have gone*. We could ask him 'Which negative preterite form of *dare* do you use?' Many difficulties arise, no doubt beginning with the need to explain what 'negative preterite' means, but not ending there. It is not merely difficult to introspect about one's own use of language: it is also difficult to control one's motives in selecting an answer to a question about language. People are quite liable to give you not the form they think they use but the one they think they ought to use and the one they would like you to think they used. Similarly, a direct question of opinion on *He would have liked to have gone* is likely to be answered with a wary thought about giving a 'received' answer. There are ways of avoiding the introspection difficulty: one can say, for example, 'Which do you prefer, *He didn't dare go* or *He dared not go* or *He didn't dare to go*?' But one is left with the imponderable about the genuineness or sincerity of the answer. What is needed is some way of eliciting the person's natural use of a form or his reaction to it without his having to indulge in either introspection or doubts about correctness. Let us suppose we have persuaded him to change all the positive sentences we utter into negative ones, and we then ask him to give the negative forms of *He is happy*, *He hated working*, *He dared to answer her back*, and *He would have liked to have gone*. In the first two, there is virtually no choice and in the third it is likely that he will respond equally automatically with his habitual, natural form. In the fourth, he may answer *He wouldn't have liked to go* if that is the form that comes more naturally to him, and even if he feels obliged to reiterate the sentence as closely as possible to the original, it is likely that he will stumble or hesitate slightly if it is not for him the natural way of saying it. A single individual's responses are, of course, little help, but by using a test technique on these lines with groups of students and teachers, we are able to elicit information on doubtful points with great speed and in large quantities, and in mass tests of this sort, even slight hesitations from half a dozen people can be sufficient clue to the tendency towards unacceptability.

With these truncated and inadequate remarks on the linguistic branch of the tree diagram, I should like to devote a little time to the computational branch. It appears to be in the nature of language that the units which we isolate in order to describe regularities (units such as the parts of speech, word, clause, sentence) are not discrete like the component parts of a machine, but are rather clusters of properties, closely associated at the centre, variable and more loosely associated at the periphery, at which point one finds properties associated with other clusters.[3] To give a single example, there is the gradient from preposition to noun phrase that we have in a series like *by*, *beside*, *by the side of*, *at the newly-restored north side of*. Then again, it appears to be in the nature of language *use* that our selection of a given linguistic form is complicatedly influenced by a host of factors such as neighbouring linguistic structures, the emphasis we wish to convey, the occasion on which we are discoursing, and the subject matter of our discourse. To plot all the properties and record all the variable factors that may be relevant and then to chart their co-occurrences must inevitably be extremely arduous, and in

---

[3] Cf. H. T. Carvell and J. Svartvik, *Computational Experiments in Grammatical Classification* (The Hague 1967), especially Ch. 10.

practice linguists have found it impossible, being obliged instead to rely on partial analyses illuminated by intuition. We are not yet within sight of the time when partial human analyses can be superseded, still less of the time when intuition will cease to be a guiding light, but the electronic computer can take over a great deal of the repetitive drudgery and can effect a richer correlation of data than has ever been possible in the past.

Current work in association with the Survey is aimed at automation, not of the basic analytical work, but of the work of collating analysed material.[4] The principle is simple enough, however great be the problems of putting it into practice. We can feed into the permanent store of the computer three types of data. The first is an appropriately-coded version of the texts in the Survey corpus; this involves only the long and careful labour of punching holes in paper tape according to the code for the particular letters and punctuation marks, together with 'location marker' signs at regular intervals, uniquely specifying each stretch of language. Secondly, a structural description of these stretches of language is punched up, together with the corresponding location markers. This structural description has been prepared by a linguist and embodies just such of the properties and factors mentioned earlier as, in his judgement, are likely to be linguistically relevant; there is theoretically no limit on the degree of detail that he may wish to specify. Thirdly, a computational expert supplies a precise description of the structural description itself. This is, so to say, a 'grammar' of the symbology used in the structural description.

Let us consider the procedure in relation to a couple of examples:

(1) the discount on security sterling which dealers were offering (should be . . .)
(2) (. . . liked) the belt with silver studs that this girl was flaunting

It will be agreed that, along with a great deal of lexical difference and some grammatical difference, there is important similarity in these two phrases. Let us suppose that they are part of the corpus encoded in the computer store, and let us further suppose that the linguist has decided on a structural description that will

---

[4] This part of the project is now directed by Geoffrey N. Leech at the University of Lancaster.

ignore the lexical differences but is able to register some of the grammatical differences. The corresponding descriptions might then be as follows:

(1a) S/TH (1 P/NH/) (C/Hwh/ S/Hs/ 2 f)/
(2a) C/TH (1 P/NHs/) (C/Hwh/ S/TH/ 2 f)/

A string of symbols can easily look alarming, but these reflect no special sophistication of analysis. The initial S and C stand for 'subject' and 'complement' respectively; T stands for the closed system of determiners of which *the* may be regarded as the chief member, mutually exclusive with *a*, *this*, *that*; H stands for 'head', the element in the structure which determines concord, for example. The similarity in the strings of symbols (1a) and (2a) reflects the similarity which the linguist chooses to see in the two structures (1) and (2). But it should be observed that he has chosen also to see differences: he sees, for instance, that in the relative clauses, the head of the subject group in one is plural and not preceded by an article, while in the other it is not plural but has an article. On the other hand, he has equally chosen to ignore differences: most obviously, he ignores the widespread difference in word-selection (*discount* in the first and *belt* in the second are alike denoted simply as 'H', for example), and he uses a symbol 'Hwh' which in one case denotes *which* and in the other *that*. Only later work with the material will confirm or question the rightness of his decision in these respects, but before we ask what this later work may be, we must add a word on the third type of data fed into the permanent store of the computer.

The 'grammar' of the structural description will be an inventory of the symbols used, grouping them in sets with an explanation of the way they are used and the combinations into which they can enter. It will be necessary to show that the oblique strokes and the parentheses are in pairs, and that an opening oblique is recognizable by one of a specified set of prefixes, that the next is the closing one unless another of these prefixes intervenes, and that the closures operate concentrically, from inward to outward. By the same token, this grammar shows how the dominant H (one of four in each of our examples) is to be recognized as such, and specifies the range and type of symbol-denoted structures that may cluster round each H and be related to the dominant one. Thus, a part of this account of the structural description (where R = 'recursive', R* = 'repeatable', and K = 'formal item to be enumerated') might read:

(3) R [FORM] = [PREMODS] [CENTRE] [POST-MODS]
(4) R [CENTRE] = [NUCLEUS] [[&] [NUCLEUS] R*], [HEAD]
(5) R [NUCLEUS] = ([FORM])
(6) K [HEAD] = H, Hs

Let us suppose, by way of explanation, that we have a noun phrase rather simpler than (1) or (2), 'the lively band that gave such pleasure'; (3) would operate on the structural description of this so as to divide it into three parts:

(3a) [the lively] [band] [that gave such pleasure]

and (4) would identify the centre (the second of these parts) as simply a head, so that (6) would cause the enumeration of the linguistic item *band*. But at the point in noun phrase structure where we have *band* in this example, we might have had a co-ordinated string of items like

(4a) (... lively) [band,] [(and) choir,] [and morris dancers] (that ...)

In such a case, (4) would identify this centre not as head but as a string of nuclei. And since each such nucleus has some potentiality for modification itself, as in

(5a) (... choir and) [morris] [dancers] [in gay costumes] (that gave ...)

it is necessary that (5) should be recursive and refer each nucleus back to (3) for an analysis of its form.

We come now to the 'later work with the material' mentioned above: what work and how is it carried out? With the three sets of data in the computer store, we can feed in 'programs' with several important capacities. There must be an 'analyser' which will interpret the structural descriptions in terms of the stored 'grammar' (1a and 2a, for example, in terms of 3, 4, 5, 6), so that all the components and their interrelationships are recognized. There must be the capacity to associate the structural descriptions with the correct textual segments (1a and 2a, for example, with 1 and 2 respectively), by means of the corresponding location markers. We require also the ability to understand and answer questions about structural descriptions.

Thus we might ask for all complements in sentence structure to be printed out; this would involve scanning all structural descriptions for sequences with the superordinate prefix C (such as (2b)), for these to be matched with the corresponding segments in the textual data, and for stretches like (2)—but not (1)—to be printed out. Such a task in itself would not, of course, be very informative, but even so, if we had not already suspected it, this might be the beginning of the interesting observation that far more noun phrases with the degree of complexity shown in (1) and (2) occur as complements than as subjects. If we had already suspected precisely this, we might alternatively have asked for all noun phrases of a certain minimum degree of complexity as in

(7) / . . .H . . .(. . .) (. . .). . ./

to be counted with a print-out of the totals according as the prefix was S or C, together with location markers. This might take us some way towards establishing the kind of English—relatively technical and relatively uncolloquial like (1) in contrast to (2)—in which such heavily modified sentence-subjects occur most naturally.

It will be noted that the question facilities have an important flexibility in enabling the collation and comparison process to ignore or take account of features in a structural description. Thus in the light of structures like

(8) the belt that this girl was wearing with the silver studs
    /   (   )(   )/
(9) the belt with the silver studs that she'd sharpened slightly
    /   (   )/

which are different from each other and from the structure common to (1) and (2), it would clearly be of interest to investigate the types of postmodification found in the corpus, perhaps by asking first for a classified print-out of noun phrases which have the element 'Hwh' in their structure.

It is unsatisfactory to attempt in one brief lecture an account of something as complex as an investigation into people's knowledge of their own language. Such an account must inevitably be oversimplified or disjointedly obscure, or both. But the attempt in the present instance is, perhaps, especially unsatisfactory in that I have had to confine my remarks to the work being done on this subject by a handful of busy colleagues in the Survey of English Usage at University College London. The story would have been much more interesting if I could have related this to the work in this same field being done in numerous universities in several countries. And the story would have gained an essential perspective if due acknowledgement had been made of the way in which all work on English grammatical usage has been illuminated by the ferment of ideas in general linguistics over the past dozen years. The extent to which this account is the product of collaboration with my colleagues on the Survey must at least be made clear, however, even if I cannot show out wider debt to colleagues in other fields, in other places, and, indeed, in other ages.

Index